Dollhouse Style

Dollhouse Style

Kath Dalmeny

RUNNING PRESS
PHILADELPHIA • LONDON

Library of Congress Cataloging-in-Publication
Number 2002100442

ISBN 0-7624-1325-5

Conceived, designed, and produced by
Quarto Publishing plc
The Old Brewery
6 Blundell Street
London N7 9BH

QUAR.DOLL

Senior Project Editor Tracie Lee Davis
Art Editor Karla Jennings
Designer Paul Wood
Assistant Art Director Penny Cobb
Illustrators Elsa Godfrey, Sally Launder
Photographers Colin Bowling, Paul Forrester
Editor Jan Cutler
Picture Researchers Sandra Assersohn,
  Penny Cobb, Kath Dalmeny
Proofreader Anne Plume

Art Director Moira Clinch
Publisher Piers Spence

Manufacturered by
Pica Digital Pte., Ltd., Singapore

Printed by
Leefung-Asco Printers Ltd., China

contents

introduction

Planning a dollhouse interior is an adventure into history. A plain room can be transformed in so many ways, each choice taking you into a new and fascinating story from the past. The secret of historical accuracy lies in the attention to detail. Wall coverings, flooring, textiles, furniture, and accessories all carry information about the lifestyles and expectations of the people who made them and lived with them. It is this essence of history in miniature that this book seeks to explore.

The book is divided into 15 chapters, each discussing a classic interior from an especially interesting period. Throughout the book, interiors have been chosen that demonstrate hallmark features of the period style, and projects that can easily be translated into your own dollhouse room. You may choose to follow the instructions and tips to create complete interiors, or you may choose to create individual items to add to your own collection. In each chapter, useful historical advice will help you to choose items and materials most suited to your own dollhouse world.

Throughout history, dolls and miniatures have always been popular. The fascination lies in recreating aspects of contemporary life, recording the details of existence at a particular time. In very early history, dolls may have been used as charms or mementoes of family members. In later centuries, miniature people had religious significance, and were treated with great reverence and symbolism—some homes having miniature scenes set up as shrines, the dolls arranged to represent important scenes from religious history.

In more modern times, miniature scenes and dollhouses have taken on practical and playful roles. During the 17th and 18th centuries, grand cabinet dollhouses, especially impressive Dutch examples, were often used to help educate young girls in the finer details of managing a household. Marrying in their early teens, they would already need to be proficient in managing linen supplies, maintaining a well-stocked larder, and keeping within a strict budget. Having played with this world

in miniature, guided by an experienced older sister or their mother, they would be well prepared to take on this adult role.

Modern dollhouses are also about escapism and the playful living out of decorative fantasies. Few of us can expect to live in a stately home, yet we can bring this world into our own lives by recreating it in miniature. The fun lies in finding ways to represent historical items in miniature using everyday tools and materials.

In this book, Dollhouse Style, a tour of history will take you from a stately Tudor banqueting hall, through grand interiors of the 17th and 18th centuries, to domestic 19th century rooms, an American small-town store, and through into striking

modern designs for a Frank Lloyd Wright sitting room, a 1950s American diner, and a modern warehouse-conversion apartment. At every stage, you will find out how to choose the materials and techniques best suited to the period style.

Whether you wish to create a simple project such as a vase of flowers, or a more complicated item such as a chair or desk, full templates and instructions have been provided. For beginners, basic techniques such as how to use templates, tools and materials are included on pages 8 to 13.

Whatever your choice of historical period, use this book to add to your repertoire of skills and understanding of historical detail, to help bring your own dollhouse collection to life.

Tools, materials, and
techniques

A well-stocked toolbox is the essential starting point for creating the miniature projects described in this book. On these pages, you can find descriptions of many of the tried and trusted tools that will prove most useful in creating your 1:12 scale craft projects. It is well worth investing in high-quality tools that will stand the test of time. A plane, saws and craft knives with fine cutting blades, replaced or sharpened frequently, will be a joy to work with and ensure precise edges for a neat finish. Different grades of sandpaper will also help you to give wooden items a beautifully smooth surface ready for a final coat of paint or varnish. When your tool collection is complete, pick a storage box with both large and small compartments, to help you sort your tools, materials and tiny components into good order. Whatever your choice of project or technique, choosing the right tools, and using high-quality items will set you off on the right course for satisfying craft work.

A plane is a useful tool for smoothing flat wooden surfaces.

Ready-made dollhouse items can be used as components of larger projects.

MAKING HOLES

▶ DRILL
An electric or hand drill can be used for making circular holes, decorative holes, and circular slots in which to secure the legs of a stool. Invest in a set of miniaturist's drill bits that will provide a range of sizes.
Frequently used sizes are:
⅛ in. (3mm);
5/16 in. (8mm);
1/16 in. (2mm);
3/16 in. (5mm);
1/32 in.(1mm).

▼ AWL
When inserting screws or nails you can make a preliminary hole by using a sharp awl. A preliminary hole will help guide the screw or nail into the material at the correct angle. When working with wood, it will also help you avoid splitting the wood when the screw or nail is inserted.

GLUING AND HOLDING

▶ GLUE
White glue is used for most projects described in this book, as it is suitable for materials such as wood, paper, and cardboard. Impact adhesive or a hot glue gun has been specified for those projects where glue is required to set more rapidly.

CUTTING AND SHAPING

▼ KNIVES

For most projects in this book, a fine craft knife with a flexible blade is suitable for cutting out shapes from paper, cardboard, and thin wood. Replace the blades frequently to ensure that they are very sharp, to keep your shaping accurate. For safety, always cut in the direction away from your hands and body. A sturdy craft knife with a strong blade is also useful for cutting out large pieces and straight edges.

▶ METAL RULER

Use a metal ruler for cutting straight edges. Its resilient edge will not be damaged when a sharp knife is drawn along it and will give an accurate cut line. Plastic rulers tend to deteriorate when used in this way. Metal rulers that have a rubber underside are especially useful, as they grip well without slipping. To cut a straight edge, line up the metal ruler with the pencil line that is drawn on the wood or paper. Draw the knife along the edge of the ruler, allowing the tip to press down into the material. Repeat until you have cut all the way through.

▼ SAWS

For thicker pieces of wood you will need to use an electric jigsaw or a tenon saw (*left*) for cutting straight lines. Use an electric jigsaw or a coping saw (*below*) for complicated curves and shapes.

MITER BLOCK

A miter block is a very useful tool for helping you to cut accurate mitered corners, when fitting skirting board to the corners of a room or when making picture frames.

▶ SCISSORS

Paper and cardboard can quickly blunt good-quality fabric scissors so it is well worth keeping more than one pair of scissors and allocating them dedicated uses. To remind family and friends to stick to the rules, you could attach labels to the different pairs of scissors describing their dedicated function.

▲ PENCIL

Use a sharp pencil to draw around a template or to draw guidelines onto wood, paper, plastic, or fabric. Choose one with a hard lead, such as an H or 2H, to ensure the minimum of damage to the surface of your materials.

◀ CHISELS

The two most useful chisels for a miniaturist's toolbox are a narrow flat-ended chisel for making shallow cuts, such as slots, and a small scoop-ended chisel for shaping curves and points. It is also useful to have a chisel sharpener, such as a sharpening stone, to keep the blades in good condition.

▶ CUTTING MAT

All cutting should take place either with the piece held in a vise or against a mat designed to protect your work surface. Cutting mats are available from art and craft stores. They provide a resilient, self-healing surface.

◀ VISE

A vise can be fitted to the side of your worktable. Use it to keep pieces together while the glue dries, for steadying work while you cut it, and for holding items steady as you add fine paint details.

◀ CLAMPS AND CLIPS

When working at a tiny scale, holding pieces steady enough to work on them is a constant challenge. Many tools are available to help ease this problem, including this unusual set of crocodile clips mounted onto adjustable arms. Some versions of this tool are available with a magnifying-glass attachment to give you a really close-up view.

▶ TAPE

When assembling the components of an item of miniature furniture, it is sometimes easiest to secure one piece on to a surface with some tape while you glue the other pieces in position. This technique can also be used to hold the doors of a cabinet in place while you attach the hinges.

FINISHING

▶ RASP

A flat-edged or mouse-tail rasp has a stiff, abrasive edge and is used for adjusting the shape of awkward corners in wooden items. Rub the rasp fairly gently backward and forward in the problem area to remove any unwanted wood.

◀ SANDPAPER

It is essential to use sandpaper to achieve a beautiful finish, especially on wooden items. Start with coarse sandpaper to smooth off rough edges caused by sawing. When the edges and surface feel smooth, switch to a finer grade and repeat. Any staining or varnishing is best done soon after sanding to give the cleanest, neatest finish.

◀ PAINT AND VARNISH

Many different paints can be used to decorate and finish furniture and accessories. Acrylic, gouache, oil-based, and enamel paints are suitable for many of the items appearing in this book. To finish your work, acrylic or oil-based varnishes are used on most of the items; they are available in matte (dull) or gloss (shiny) finishes. Take care when choosing a varnish: some may spoil certain types of painted surface. Some oil-based varnishes, for example, will dissolve metallic enamel paints, and some acrylic or water-based varnishes will affect acrylic or water-based paints. When varnishing painted or decorated surfaces prepare a test piece made with the same materials, then varnish a sample area and leave to dry. Check to ensure that the colors and textures remain satisfactory. If not, test another area with a different varnish.

▶ PAINTBRUSHES

A range of paintbrushes can fulfill a variety of functions and help you achieve different paint effects. For fine detail, choose a small brush with a pointed end. To cover large areas, choose a wide, flat brush. To create a stippled paint effect, choose a small brush with bristles cut short to give a flat end. Whatever the paint used, always wash brushes thoroughly after use, following the paint manufacturer's instructions. Some paints wash off with water whereas others require special chemicals or treatment.

MATERIALS

▲ READY-MADE FLOURISHES AND EDGINGS

Ready-made flourishes and edgings, sold as architectural details by dollhouse suppliers, are available in plastic and plaster finishes. These can be cut and painted to fit in your dollhouse interior.

▲ BEADS

Beads come in a surprising variety of shapes and sizes. Look out for shapes that can be used as the feet or handles of furniture and accessories.

▶ ALUMINUM STRIP

Aluminum strip, available from specialist modeling stores, is useful for modern fixtures and fittings, such as the trimmings in a 1950s American Diner.

▶ COLORED PAPER AND CARDBOARD

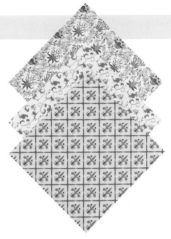

A range of colored paper and cardboard will prove an invaluable resource for any miniaturist. It can be used for projects as diverse as wall coverings and flowers, such as the paper sunflowers on page 97.

◀ READY-MADE PLASTER PIECES

To create three-dimensional features in a room, such as pillars, porticos, and decorative wall brackets, choose ready-made plasterwork pieces that can be left plain or embellished with gold-painted details.

▶ DOWELING

Wooden doweling can be used as furniture legs, handles and items such as handrails in many dollhouse settings. Colored with paint or stain, it can be transformed to give various finishes.

PERSPEX TUBE

Narrow Perspex tube can be cut into short lengths for miniature tumblers, to be filled with colorful polymer clay to mimick orange juice or cocktails.

PERSPEX

Modern materials such as see-through plastic strips can be used to mimic glass shelves and Perspex pillars for modern interiors and 1:12-scale stores and restaurants.

◀ ALUMINUM ROD

Rods made from aluminum are strong and give a characteristic modern look for use in contemporary scenes. Once in place, fingerprints and smudges can be cleaned off using regular furniture polish.

▼JEWELRY FITTINGS

Tiny brass rings cut from a toy necklace, or purchased from a jewelry supplier, can be used as the handles of modern furniture.

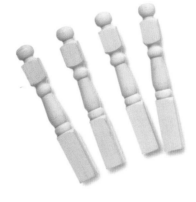

▲RIBBONS AND FABRICS

Look out for ribbons and close-weave fabrics with attractive colors and patterns to enliven your dollhouse room. These ribbons can be used for curtain tie-backs, rug edgings, and cushion covers.

►JEWELRY PINS

Specialist jewelry components such as these pins can provide useful lengths of fine-grade silver and brass wire for creating miniature fittings.

►WIRE

Fine wire available from modeling stores and floristry suppliers is useful for creating fine shapes such as the curved stems of a trailing plant.

◄MODELING CLAY

Polymer modeling clay is available in many useful colors for miniature modeling. It is easy to form into detailed shapes and can be baked in a domestic oven to harden the clay and make the shapes permanent.

BANISTERS

Ready-turned and shaped dollhouse banisters are a valuable source of decoratively shaped wooden strip, from which to cut sections for furniture legs, handles, or trimming.

DOLLHOUSE SCALE

One-twelfth scale is the most popular scale for dollhouses. To copy an item from real life, make measurements of the original full-scale item and divide each measurement by 12. The new measurement is the one to use for cutting pieces to create your miniature item. A pocket calculator will prove invaluable in making these calculations. The models and templates in this book have been prepared in 1:12 scale.

▲NEWEL POSTS

Newel posts are a stylish finishing point for a stairway handrail. Or use these ready-made pieces as components for larger dollhouse projects.

►BRASS FIXTURES AND FITTINGS

Miniature brass fixtures and fittings are available from specialist dollhouse suppliers. Used as door handles, hinges, and decorative flourishes, they bring a professional finish to hand-made dollhouse items.

▼WOOD STRIP

Strips of wood, available from specialist dollhouse suppliers, can be used for creating many of the wooden items described in this book. Here, pine strips, glued side by side, mimic tongue-and-groove paneling.

►PLASTER MOLDINGS

Ready-made plaster moldings make fine finishing touches to a grand dollhouse interior, used as chair rails and cornice pieces.

TECHNIQUES

USING TEMPLATES

The templates provided in this book are actual size unless otherwise stated. Trace or photocopy the template onto paper and cut it out around the black solid line. Use a craft knife to cut out any gray shapes marked on the template. Place the template onto the material—usually wood—described in the instructions, then draw around it with a sharp pencil. Mark the positions of any gray shapes on the template. Remove the template and use an appropriate tool to cut out the shape.

▶ Some templates have areas marked in gray, showing the positions for cutting slots or making holes.

CUTTING OUT WOODEN SHAPES

An electric jigsaw or a tenon saw are suitable for cutting straight lines. For complicated shapes, hold the piece in a vise and use an electric jigsaw or a coping saw to cut away spare wood. Use a craft knife to cut pieces from very thin or very soft wood. Start by drawing around the edge of the shape with the point of the knife. Re-cut into the line again and again until you have cut all the way through.

▲ To hold the piece steady, clamp it in a vise then cut out the shape carefully using an electric jigsaw or a coping saw.

MAKING SLOTS

For many dollhouse accessories and items of furniture described in this book, glue will be strong enough to keep the pieces together and in shape. For larger or more complicated items of furniture, you will need to cut slots to give the components a stronger connection. To cut a slot, use a sharp craft knife to mark out the edges of the slot shape, as described in the text or shown in gray on the template. Use a small, flat chisel or craft knife to pick out the wood in the center of the slot.

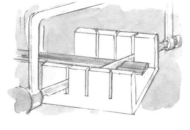

▲ A small flat-ended chisel is useful for removing wood from the middle of a slot.

CUTTING MITERED CORNERS

Where pieces of wood meet at a right-angled corner—such as skirting board at the corner of a room, or pieces of molding fitted together as a picture frame—they will fit together neatly if each is cut at a 45° angle, called a miter. A miter block is a very useful tool for helping you to cut accurate miter corners. Place the piece of wood flush with the inside wall of the block. Fit the blade of a tenon saw into the 45° angle and cut the wood, keeping the saw within the slot.

▲ To cut accurate 45-degree angles, a miter block is a very useful addition to the miniaturist's toolbox.

GLUING PIECES TOGETHER

When you use glue that takes a few minutes or even hours to dry, hold the glued components together in a clamp or vise. For delicate surfaces that may be damaged by the pressure place soft material, such as felt, around the item before holding it in the vise, but make sure that the fabric is kept well clear of the glue. Alternatively, wind a rubber band temporarily around the item, gently pulling the glued edges together. Leave to dry thoroughly.

◀ Pieces of an item can be held together either in a vise or with rubber bands while the glue dries. Instructions for this chair are on page 98.

CARVING A PATTERNED SURFACE

A sharp knife or chisel can be used to carve attractive stylized designs on wooden items. Use the point of the blade to mark out the edges of the design. For an outline design, run the knife blade around the design again, a little outside the initial cut, with the blade pointing down into the initial cut. Remove any loose wood with the knife. For a design where some areas are deeper than others, outline the design in the same way as before, and then use a narrow chisel to remove wood in the chosen areas.

▶ A sharp knife or chisel can be used to carve attractive stylized designs on wooden items. Instructions for this Bible box are on page 76.

MAKING LATTICE DESIGNS

Impressive latticework designs can be cut from cardboard, and then painted to give the impression of a variety of different materials. This "jade" table and the cabinet on page 108—with its latticework windows and curled top pieces—are good examples. In each case a sharp craft knife was used to cut out a shaped design from cardboard. For the cabinet, the cardboard was painted to match the cabinet. For the table, the cardboard was stippled with yellow-green paint to give the impression of jade. Instructions for the jade table are on page 45.

◀ Intricate lattices can be cut from cardboard to make an impressive design, and then painted to give the impression of wood or stone.

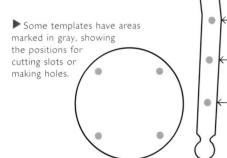

DOLLHOUSE FLOORING

Wherever possible, laying a dollhouse floor should be completed before fitting the skirting board, to give a neat finish. A number of different techniques can be used to give attractive flooring finishes.

▲ These colorful geometric floor tiles were created with a computer and color printer. See the American Diner on page 112

▲ Parquet flooring paper is available from dollhouse suppliers. See the Frank Lloyd Wright Sitting Room on page 96.

USING A PHOTOCOPIER

If you have access to a photocopier, it will prove an invaluable tool for helping you to make your miniature items.

▲ This stereo equipment can be created quite simply with a color photocopy from a catalog of electrical equipment mounted onto small cardboard boxes. See the Modern Apartment on page 131.

DOLLHOUSE WALL COVERINGS

Your choice of covering for the dollhouse walls will have an important impact on the look and period style of the whole room.

▲ Line a wall with wooden strips to give the impression of a house built from planks. See the American Settler's Parlor on page 72.

▶ Panels of brocade fabric are a beautiful addition to a room, mounted onto the wall and framed with strips of molding. See the 1920s' Living Room on page 104.

▲ A laptop computer can be made from two pieces of cardboard hinged together, covered with the laptop template photocopied from the Modern Apartment on page 131.

◀ The miniature newspaper in the American Diner on page 117 was created by reducing a real newspaper page on a photocopier to the appropriate size.

DOLLHOUSE WINDOWS

In some historical settings, stained glass windows or windows with patterned tracery help to capture the period style.

▲ Tracery can be drawn onto the window's Perspex or glass with a permanent felt-tip pen. See the American Settler's Parlor on page 75.

PAINT EFFECTS

Structures made from cardboard, wood, paper, or plaster can be transformed to give the impression of other materials by using clever paint effects.

▲ To give a stone effect, create stone shapes from air-drying clay on a floor or fireplace. Stipple the dried clay with acrylic paints. See the American Settler's Parlor on page 76.

◀ For marble, cover a fireplace with marbled paper or drag lines of white and ochre acrylic paint through a dark painted surface while it is still wet. See the Lying-in Room on page 24.

DOLLHOUSE WINDOWS (continued)

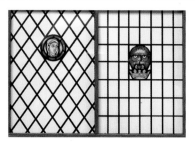

▲ To incorporate a colored panel, prepare the window design on paper and then photocopy it onto thin plastic to be mounted into the window frame. See the Tudor Banqueting Hall on page 21.

▶ For a stained-glass effect, black lines can be drawn with a permanent marker, and panes can be picked out with colored permanent felt-tip pens or specialist transparent glass paint. See the Frank Lloyd Wright Sitting Room on page 100.

EMBROIDERY

A touch of embroidery worked in tiny stitches can transform items in a dollhouse room. Choose colors and materials carefully to suit the period style.

▼ Cushions in a seventeenth-century Lying-in Room will look beautiful with the addition of just a few embroidered flowers worked in white silk. See page 27.

▶ Geometric blackwork designs worked on counted-thread embroidery fabric are suitable for a Tudor Banqueting Hall. See page 20.

the designs

This book is divided into 15 different historical scenes that illustrate the changing uses and fashions of rooms from the 16th century to the present day. For each period, a classic dollhouse scene is pictured, chosen from beautiful examples on display in historical collections, and in some cases recreated especially for this book. Each chapter breaks down the scene into its key elements, explaining what furniture, accessories, tools, and materials you can use to recreate the items for your own collection. Six classic projects in each chapter are described in even more detail, with step-by-step instructions to guide you through the stages of constructing the items. Sometimes advice is also given for adapting ready-made furniture to fit with your chosen period style. Throughout, the emphasis is on the fun and fascination of creating historical worlds in miniature, taking a simple dollhouse room as your starting point.

Tudor banqueting hall

Furniture and fittings in a sixteenth-century, English Tudor room were built to last. Indeed such was the commitment to the longevity of buildings that sometimes when a hall was built, acorns were planted nearby to provide timber for the future. Centuries later, when the ceiling beams finally lost their strength, new wood was available to repair the roof and keep the building in good order.

The banqueting hall of a Tudor manor house was used for feasts, celebrations, and entertainment. Often the hall would resound with the stories of hunting exploits, or the long benches would be filled with the family of the household listening to music or the poetry and songs of traveling players. Whatever the activity, the banqueting hall was the heart of the household and usually the place to display hunting trophies and armor, demonstrating to guests the family's prowess and noble ancestry. This pride in family history was also displayed in crests and on shields, or could be incorporated into the designs of stained-glass windows. In this chapter, classic projects from the Tudor period have been described to enable you to bring this air of history and nobility to your own dollhouse.

A simple Tudor chair.

THE BASICS

◄ MAKING A FLOOR

The floors of many Tudor halls were made of slabs of local stone. Press out a layer of air-drying clay over the whole floor area and use the edge of a piece of cardboard to mark out the lines of the slabs. Near the doorway, make a shallow dip in the stone where many feet have worn it away over the years. When hardened, stipple the slabs with acrylic paint, using mainly gray but dabbing in a little brown and ochre to soften the effect. Seal with matte varnish. Alternatively, cover the whole floor with stone-effect paper, available from most dollhouse suppliers.

◄ THE WALLS

A striking feature common in Tudor houses is the use of carved oak paneling on the walls. A popular design involved low-relief carving imitating the folds of cloth, now known as linen-fold paneling. At the time, this pattern was called *lignum undulatum*, which translates as wavy woodwork. The panels in the scene have been hand carved, but you could also mimic the effect by cutting wavy-edged scroll pieces from brown corrugated craft cardboard. Mount on a square of card and frame with strips, then glue the panels in rows on the wall.

▼ DISPLAY SHELF

Above the wooden paneling, fit a small shelf to display hunting trophies and pewter plates; a shallow groove cut into the shelf surface will stop the plates from slipping off. To hold up the shelf, glue lengths of ½ in. (12mm) wood strip to the wall. Secure the shelf on top. Triangular supports, cut from ready-shaped wood molding, can be glued at regular intervals, fitting snugly into the angle between the shelf and the wall.

FURNITURE AND FITTINGS

▼ CHAIR AND BENCH

To signify his status, the head of this household sat on a sturdy upright chair with the women and children sitting on the plain benches on either side of the table. The family's food would have been served by servants. This chair and bench are constructed quite simply from blocks of wood jointed together. In keeping with the wealthy yet restrained style of the room, they have just a touch of decorative detail in the shaping of the legs and in the carving on the back of the chair.

▶ FIREPLACE

A stone floor and a high ceiling lend an austere and chilly quality to a room, making the fireplace a focal point as the main source of color and warmth. The fireplace is built from wood, with wooden molding used to create the carved edges, and finished with textured, stone-effect paint (see instructions on page 19).

PLATES AND BOWLS

Cast metal plates, goblets and serving dishes are available from dollhouse suppliers, or can be made by coating ready-made plastic items with metallic pewter enamel paint. Wooden bowls can be made from large coat buttons. Fill the holes with air-drying clay, and when dry, cover the clay with acrylic paint.

LIGHTING

The main sources of light are the fire and candles. Wall-mounted candles with flame-effect bulbs are available from specialist suppliers and should be planned and fitted at the same time as the paneling, following the manufacturer's instructions, so that the modern cables can be hidden behind the wood finish.

▶ BANQUET

Everyday food involved simple fare such as bread, cheese, apples, and beer. For a banquet, use polymer clay to make grapes to fill a bowl, and model roasted chickens or pheasants. Once the models of the birds are baked and hard, give the effect of roasting by stippling the top surface of each with ochre acrylic paint, add a little brown and stipple again. Finally, add a little black to the paint mix and stipple the most prominent surfaces of each bird, where it might have been burnt while being roasted.

▶ CHEST

Essential to any large house, this chest might contain folded embroidered linen that is stored away for special occasions. Built from panels of wood, with tiny brass hinges held in place by pins, it is decorated with the same elegant motif as the chair. You might choose to create your own family crest or motif to appear on these items. Popular motifs included lions, unicorns, roses, foliage, and bees, to symbolize qualities such as strength, natural beauty, and hard work. Instructions are on page 18.

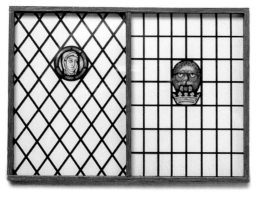

▼ TABLE

A long rectangular table dominated the banqueting hall, using planks from an ancient oak tree to support the weight of an extravagant feast. The table was placed in the center of the room, and the feast was a symbol to guests of the wealth and generosity of the family.

▶ SOFT FURNISHINGS

Clothing and soft furnishings were embellished with geometric or floral designs worked in black silk on a linen background. Pillows, bed hangings, drapes, cuffs and collars, all carried the characteristic patterns. The counted-thread design on page 20 is adapted from an original pattern depicted by the painter Hans Holbein.

ADD TO THE LOOK

▶ WINDOWS

Large panes of glass were difficult to manufacture and expensive to replace, so windows of this period were made up of small rectangular or diamond-shaped panes held in place by lead tracery. Using modern techniques and materials, it is possible to copy leaded windows at a miniature scale, even adding panels to mimic stained glass. Instructions are on page 21.

The occupants of this grand hall would have spent many of their days hunting in the extensive grounds. Trophies from their exploits would include the heads of animals such as deer and boars. The bear head in this model has been cut from a plastic toy animal and mounted on to a display board. A template for the board is on page 19. See pages 10–13 for tips on using templates.

BENCH

This household's furniture is simple yet sturdy, embellished with touches of carving. The finish is slightly rough, revealing the use of hand-held tools. This effect is mimicked in miniature by running a craft-knife blade along the edges of the pieces to give an irregular edge. Choose a strong wood with a fine grain. Color with a dark oak stain.

❶ From ⅛ in. (3mm) thick wood cut the following:
Seat: 1 piece, 1 x 6 in. (25 x 152mm)
Upper supports: 4 pieces, each 2½ x ¼ in. (65 x 6mm) and 2 pieces, each ½ x ¼ in. (12 x 6mm)

❷ Use a craft knife to score a line down the center of the seat. Run the knife at an angle down the side of the line to slice off a little of the wood. Repeat on the other side and along the outer edges. Stain the seat and leave it to dry.

❸ From ready-turned dollhouse banisters cut six legs, 1 in. (25mm) in length. (You can choose a height to suit the design of your pieces.) Use a craft knife to trim the ends of the legs flat. Stain the legs and upper supports.

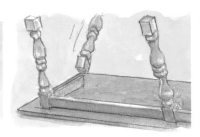

❹ Glue the upper supports and legs to the underside of the seat as shown in the diagram, making one side at a time and allowing the glue to dry between stages.

❺ From ⅛ in. (3mm) square section wood strip cut lengths to fit between the legs at the base. Stain the pieces (seven in total). Glue in position. Bind thread around the six legs to hold the bench together securely while the glue dries.

CHEST

Sometimes small and plain for holding spices, sometimes large and grandly painted with scenes of courtly life for holding precious items, a wooden chest was a common sight in the Tudor household. With its feet raising it above the floor to avoid the damp, it could also double up as a seat. It does not have a lock, as this chest was probably for everyday use as a linen store. These instructions show you how to transform a plain chest to one with patterned panels. The box is approximately 3 in. (75mm) wide by 1½ in. (38mm) tall.

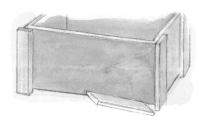

❶ Remove the lid and hinges from the box. From 1/16 in. (2mm) thick wood, cut eight strips, each ¼ in. (6mm) wide and as long as the height of the box plus 3/16 in. (5mm) for the feet. Using a blunt knife, score each piece with parallel lines, and then glue them in pairs to the corners of the box.

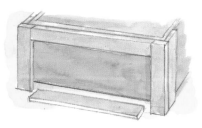

❷ Cut two strips, ¼ in. (6mm) wide and as long as the width between the two uprights. Glue to the front of the box and repeat on the other three sides.

FIREPLACE

Tudor fireplaces were built of solid stone with a deep hearth to prevent sparks from setting light to the wooden-clad walls or hanging tapestries. To complete your fireplace, cast-metal grates can be purchased from a specialist dollhouse supplier; some have a lighting effect to look like real fire. As a finishing touch, cut lengths of twig and stack them on the hearth as a supply of logs.

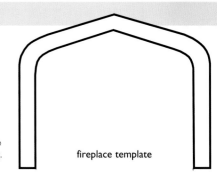
fireplace template

1 From ³⁄₁₆ in. (5mm) thick wood, cut the following:
Face: 3½ x 2⅛ in. (90 x 54mm)
Hearth: 3½ x 2 in. (90 x 50mm)
Mantelpiece: 4⅛ x 1⅜ in. (105 x 35mm)
Mantelpiece support: 3½ x 1 in. (90 x 25mm)
From ½ in. (12mm) wide wood, cut two side wall pieces, each 2⅛ in. (54mm) long.

2 Copy the fireplace frame template on to paper and cut it out. Draw around the inside of the shape on the face piece, and then use a coping saw to cut out the hole. Draw round the whole template on thick cardboard and cut it out.

3 Glue the side wall pieces to the back of the fireplace.

4 For the chimney, cut a piece of cardboard 3¼ x 2 in. (83 x 50mm). Fold a ½ in. (12mm) tab along each short edge. Glue the tabs on to the back of the face piece either side of the hole, so that the chimney is slightly curved. When dry, stick the fireplace on to the hearth, and glue the mantelpiece support on top.

5 Cut two uprights from ⅜ in. (10mm) wide molding (available as dollhouse wainscot), each 2⅛ in. (54mm) tall. Glue either side of the fireplace. Cut a length of quarter-round molding to fit under the mantelpiece support and glue it in place. Glue the mantelpiece on top. Paint the fireplace with a mix of acrylic paint, white glue, and sawdust to give texture. Sponge black paint "soot" inside the chimney.

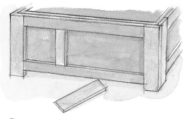

crest template

trophy template

3 Cut two strips, ¼ in. (6mm) wide to fit between the two horizontal bars. Glue to the front of the box and repeat on the other three sides. Sand the top of the box and stain.

4 Cut panels slightly smaller than the gaps between the bars. On each panel, draw the pattern, using the template as a guide. Use a craft knife to trace the line of the pattern. Trim out a little wood on either side of the line and pick out any loose wood. Stain the panels then glue in place.

5 The lid can be decorated in the same way, but because the box has become slightly bigger, let the paneling extend by ¹⁄₁₆ in. (2mm) on each side. Add thin strips of ¹⁄₁₆ in. (2mm) wood in a frame on the underside of the lid, stain the lid then reattach the hinges.

ANIMAL'S HEAD HUNTING TROPHY

To make a hunting trophy, use this template to cut a shield shape from ⅛ in. (3mm) wood. Sand the edges and stain the shield. Cut the head from a plastic zoo animal and glue it to the shield.

BLACKWORK EMBROIDERY

Embroidery known as blackwork was very popular in the sixteenth and seventeenth centuries. It was used for clothing and furnishings. The formal designs were worked on fabrics with a fairly coarse weave where threads could be counted in order to maintain a mathematical precision to the pattern. Areas were outlined in black, and then filled with formal and floral motifs of different densities to give an impression of shading. Over time the designs became more fluid, with sinuous embroidered vines and foliage twisting and overlapping around details such as collars and cuffs. Blackwork designs were mostly worked on silk or linen with black silk thread. Occasionally other colors were used, such as a striking green or red against a contrasting pale background. This project is for an embroidered cloth to protect the polished surface of a chest or side table. A portion of the design has also been adapted to create a blackwork cushion cover.

cloth stitch guide

cushion stitch guide

BLACKWORK CUSHION

For a cushion cover, work steps 1 to 4 using the square stitch guide. At step 2, also work an extra borderline around the edge. Unlike the cloth, the outer line is not required for the hem so should be worked at the embroidery stage. Cut a square of backing fabric and place the embroidery and backing fabric right sides facing. Sew them together around three edges, turn inside out and fill with stuffing or tiny scraps of fabric. Carefully tuck in the raw edges and sew closed.

BLACKWORK CLOTH

1 From a piece of 16 holes per inch (6 holes per cm) counted-thread embroidery fabric (such as Aida), cut a rectangle 4 x 2½ in. (102 x 65mm).

2 Using a single strand of black sewing thread, secure the thread, then work a line of running stitches (in and out through the fabric along a line) to define the edges of two sides of the design. Return along the lines with running stitch to fill in the spaces. Note that the outer line of the design is not worked during the embroidery stage, but is added when the piece is being hemmed. The hemline then serves as the outer line of the design.

3 Following the cloth stitch guide, start to fill in the pattern with diagonal and straight stitches. For a striking effect, add color to your embroidery by using colored embroidery floss.

4 When two sides of the pattern are finished, add the other two sides and then the central motifs. You can pick out parts of the design in different colors, then frame the design with black stitches.

5 Trim off the excess fabric, leaving a ½ in. (12mm) border. Fold under on two sides, press with a warm iron, then run a line of black stitches along each edge to hold them in place. Fold under the remaining two sides and repeat. Dab a little white glue on to the raw edges of the fabric to prevent it from fraying.

DOORWAY

1 From paper, cut an arch shape to fit across the top of the doorway. Trim until you achieve an attractive shape. Draw round the shape on to ³⁄₁₆ in. (5mm) thick wood and cut it out using a coping saw.

2 With a hard pencil, mark out the outlines and patterns shown in the picture. On each side of the pencil lines, use a sharp craft knife to make a shallow cut at a 45-degree angle. Use the point of the knife to pick out the lines of wood as they are loosened. Sand lightly, stain the piece and glue it in place.

3 Cut two strips of wood as columns for the sides of the doorway, and score them with vertical lines. Sand lightly, stain, and then glue in place.

4 Cut short lengths of broad molded dollhouse wainscot, stain them and glue them at the base of the columns.

LEADED WINDOW

Tudor windows often depicted a painted panel with a family crest or symbol. Using a photocopier (see right), you can create an impressive patterned window quite simply. Alternatively use steel wire mesh, as in the photograph above. Using pliers or metal clippers, cut a rectangle of mesh the same size as the windowpane. Slip it into position in the window and hold it in place with strips of wood. For a more authentic finish, paint the mesh black with metallic paint before fixing it in place.

1 On white paper, draw out a grid of lines with a thick black pen, larger than your window.

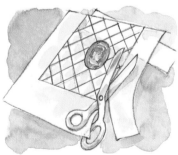

2 Cut out a small motif, glue it inside the grid and then draw a black line around it. Photocopy the design on to a heatproof plastic transparency. Cut a rectangle of the design just large enough to fit inside the window frame.

3 Secure with a tiny line of white glue around the edge, or glue strips of ⅛ in (3mm) square wood in a frame to hold it in position.

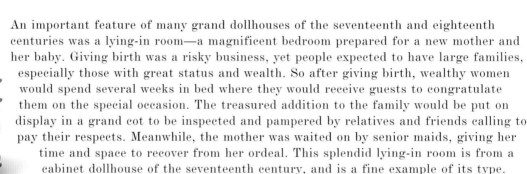

A grand cabinet provides storage space for linen and spare bedclothes.

17th-Century lying-in room

An important feature of many grand dollhouses of the seventeenth and eighteenth centuries was a lying-in room—a magnificent bedroom prepared for a new mother and her baby. Giving birth was a risky business, yet people expected to have large families, especially those with great status and wealth. So after giving birth, wealthy women would spend several weeks in bed where they would receive guests to congratulate them on the special occasion. The treasured addition to the family would be put on display in a grand cot to be inspected and pampered by relatives and friends calling to pay their respects. Meanwhile, the mother was waited on by senior maids, giving her time and space to recover from her ordeal. This splendid lying-in room is from a cabinet dollhouse of the seventeenth century, and is a fine example of its type.

A grand canopy frames the bed, endowing the mother with great status, but also giving her a little privacy and warmth. Embellished cushions were provided, upon which the new mother could be propped up to chat with guests sitting on the many chairs in the room. In this chapter, you will learn how to make many of the features to create your own elegant lying-in room.

THE BASICS

◀ MAKING A FLOOR
Large areas of polished boards could easily be swept clean, with the minimum of fuss, ensuring that the new mother and baby were disturbed as little as possible. To achieve a large area of plain wood, cover the whole floor area with good-quality plywood that has an attractive veneer as the top layer. Color with dark oak stain. For a richer effect, choose a golden stain, and varnish to finish.

▲ CEILING
The ceiling is a fine feature of this lying-in room. Bands of gilded wood frame an elaborate painting giving the impression of ornate three-dimensional leaves, swirls, and curls. On page 29, find out how to create your own ceiling with simple techniques, to replicate this impressive effect.

▶ MARBLE EFFECT FIREPLACE
A plain wooden or plasterwork fireplace can be adapted to fit into this elegant interior with the addition of a marble paint effect. Color the lower part of the fireplace with dark brown acrylic paint. While the brown is still wet, drag a paintbrush with white paint through it, leaving a trail of white. Repeat with ochre. Drag out veins of color into the brown areas. Alternatively, cover the base of the fireplace with marble-effect paper (available from bookbinding stores).

FURNITURE AND FITTINGS

▶BED
A simple wooden bed was the central feature of the room, given great status by the addition of a fine silk-satin canopy hung from a ceiling hook positioned directly above the bed. You will find instructions to make the canopy on page 26.

▶CHAIR
Furniture was light, attractive, and well made, with just a touch of decorative detail and satin cushions to make guests feel more comfortable. A set of six identical chairs is an important asset for a family welcoming visitors to the period of lying-in. Instructions for making the chair are on page 28.

▶CABINET
Linen cupboards and cabinets for storing sheets, pillowcases, and bedcovers, were standard features of a seventeenth-century lying-in room. In a time before washing machines, washdays for large fabric items were a major event, and might take place only three or four times a year. So linen was purchased in great quantities, and ample storage space was crucial.

▶COT
Family and friends would be keen to meet and admire the new baby. Placed in a satin-lined basket, the baby could be passed between the visitors to be smiled at and cooed over. Create your own cot to hold a baby doll by lining a dollhouse basket with fabric, held in place with satin ribbons. Instructions on page 27.

▲MINIATURE CHAIR
A child's wickerwork chair is an attractive addition to a lying-in room. An older child of the family would be invited to join the company and sit politely while the adults engaged in conversation. A child would be expected to behave respectfully in the presence of adults and would not be allowed to make noise or disturb the baby.

▼BASKETS
A collection of baskets makes an attractive addition to the scene. They were useful for keeping the room neat and tidy, and for carrying away dirty laundry. Baskets with small handholds at either end are the most suitable—with an open top for stacking items inside.

◀CUSHIONS
A heap of cushions on the bed were arranged so that the exhausted mother could be propped up comfortably to nurse her new baby or receive well-wishers. Cushions decorated with braids, ribbons, satin fabrics, and tassels are a lovely opportunity to introduce color and prettiness to the room. Learn how to create these cushions on page 27.

▶PICTURES AND MIRROR
Fine paintings and mirrors adorn the walls—something for the guests to admire or chat about. Paintings featuring domestic, farming, and family themes are suitable. They can be finished with gilded edging, created with strips of wooden molding, or by using ready-made plaster frames.

▶GOLDEN WALL PANEL
The decoration in this room displays great craftsmanship, but it is carefully controlled and not excessive. The branches and leaves on these beautiful golden panels are created with just a few strokes of paint, with the addition of colorful birds as a lively reminder of bountiful nature. It is a gentle theme for the mother's lying-in room, and can be re-created by following the instructions on page 29.

ADD TO THE LOOK

A collection of blue and white porcelain or blue glassware fits perfectly into this seventeenth-century scene. For porcelain, Dutch Delftware and Chinese blue and white designs were both popular. This set of blue glass may have been a congratulatory gift for the mother and new baby. Another feature commonly found in lying-in rooms was a tea set, for serving hot drinks to visitors.

BED CANOPY

A luxurious silk-satin canopy above the maternal bed served a number of functions. Because it was both labor-intensive and expensive to keep a large room heated all night, a temporary canopy over the bed helped to keep natural warmth in, creating a cozy nest for the mother and baby. In the morning, when servants and visitors arrived, the canopy drapes could be tied back and secured on the bedposts. The canopy then became a beautiful frame to the mother and baby, displaying them to their best advantage, with attractive satin ribbons enhancing the femininity of the scene.

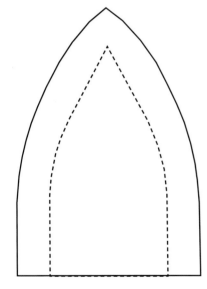

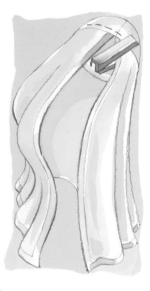

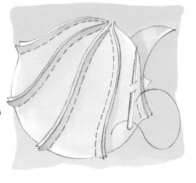

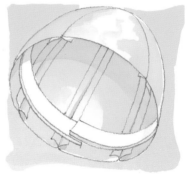

canopy head
segment template

❶ Copy the canopy head segment template onto paper and cut it out. Using a hard pencil and pressing only lightly, draw round the pattern five times on ivory-colored satin. Cut out the pieces and sew them right sides together into a cone shape, along the dotted lines marked on the pattern. Turn the piece right side out.

❷ Cut a ⅜ in. (10mm) wide, 6 ²³⁄₃₂ in. (171mm) long strip of white cardboard. Coil it around, overlapping ¼ in. (6mm) at each end, and glue it into a circle. Glue this inside the bottom edge of the canopy head, tuck the raw fabric underneath and glue it to the cardboard.

❸ Cut four drapes, each 1⅝ in. (41mm) wide and three-quarters the height of your dollhouse room. Sew ¼ in. (6mm) blue satin ribbon around two long and one short edge on each drape. Staple the top edge of each drape to the inside of the cardboard ring.

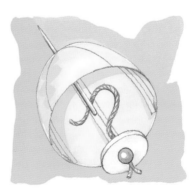

❹ Cut a 1 in. (25mm) wide, 7½ in. (190mm) long strip of satin fabric. Sew ¼ in. (6mm) blue ribbon along each edge. Make a line of running stitches down the middle and gather up the strip slightly. Run a line of quick-drying glue around the lower edge of the head section and stick the satin edging in place. Finish by gluing blue ribbon along the middle.

❺ Cut a 1¼ in. (32mm) diameter circle of white cardboard and use a thick needle to make a hole in the center. Tie a bead to a piece of gold cord and run the other end through the hole in the cardboard, then up through the center of the canopy. Thread the cord through another bead, tie the cord over a hook in the ceiling, and fasten with a knot.

❻ Gather up each drape at the corners of the bed and tie to the bedposts with pale blue satin ribbon.

LINED BASKET COT

A silk-satin-lined basket signifies the importance of a new child to the household. It is also a symbol of the luxury into which the baby was born. Tie the satin into swags, and decorate the basket with lengths of ribbon or cord, to show how much the new baby is valued, and to make a beautiful focus for the room.

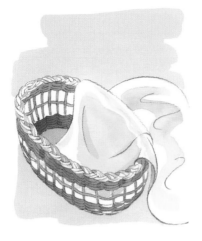

1 Choose an open basket large enough to accommodate a baby doll. Cut an oval of ivory-colored satin fabric at least 2 in. (50mm) bigger than the top of the basket. Hem the edge of the fabric and sew a line of ¼ in. (6mm) blue ribbon around the edge.

2 At intervals around the edge of the basket, use thread to gather up the fabric in broad swags. At regular intervals, sew the thread through the weave of the basket. Attach satin ribbon bows at the top point of each swag.

3 Place cushions under the satin to help support the baby. Attach ribbons to the edge of the basket to drape attractively and complete the extravagant look. Other similar baskets can be stored near the baby's basket, containing folded piles of linen, tied with white ribbons.

CUSHIONS

1 For a basic cushion, cut two pieces of fabric, each 2 in. (50mm) square. Place them right sides together and sew around three edges, leaving a ³⁄₁₆ in. (5mm) seam allowance.

2 Trim off the corners as shown in the diagram and turn right sides out. Fill the cushion with polyester toy stuffing.

3 Tuck the raw edges inside and sew the hole shut with tiny neat stitches.

TASSELS
Tassels are available from haberdashery and jewelry suppliers. Trap a tassel in each corner of the cushion seam.

EMBROIDERY
Cut a section from machine-embroidered fabric or stitch a single flower onto some fabric before making up the cushion.

RIBBONS
For a rich, decorative effect add ribbons or braid to flat fabric, and then make up the cushion following the instructions above.

LACE
Sew the edge of the lace to a finished cushion, allowing extra lace at the corners with one or two tucks, to help it lie neatly.

CHAIR

These beautiful chairs embody both simplicity and fine craftsmanship. Created on a traditional pole lathe, fine detail was not easy to create, so the carpenter made the most of the overall shape, with just a few touches of decoration in the form of round feet and ball finials. A woven seat completes the look. For the comfort of guests, add a satin cushion to the seat following the instructions on page 27.

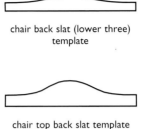

chair back slat (lower three) template

chair top back slat template

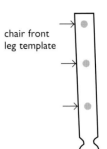

chair front leg template

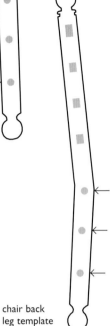

chair back leg template

1 Copy the chair templates onto paper and cut them out. Draw round each leg pattern once on ³⁄₁₆ in. (5mm) thick wood, then flip them over and draw round them again. From 2mm diameter dowel, cut 12 struts, each 1⅝ in. (41mm) long. Draw round the top back slat template once, and the lower back slats template three times on ¹⁄₁₆ in. (2mm) thick wood. Use a sharp knife to cut out the back slats, then sand the cut edges.

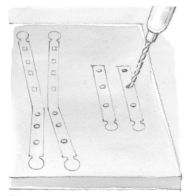

2 Before cutting out the leg pieces, tape the wood to a flat surface. Using a ¹⁄₁₆ in. (2mm) drill bit, make holes halfway through the wood in the positions marked by gray circles on the templates.

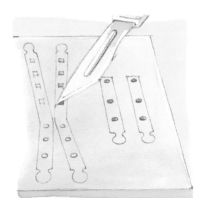

3 With a craft knife, make slots in the positions marked by gray rectangles on the back legs. Use a coping saw or miniature jigsaw to cut out the legs.

MAKING A SEAT

The woven seat is a classic feature of a fine hand-crafted seventeenth-century chair. To recreate this effect in miniature, use thread or embroidery floss in a natural brown or oatmeal color. Choose a coarser linen or button thread for a more rugged finish.

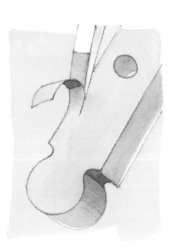

4 Use a chisel or craft knife to trim the leg pieces to a round shape, and to carve the feet and finials into balls. Finish with sandpaper.

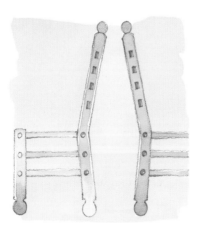

5 Compile and glue the side sections of the chair as shown in the diagram. Using a ¹⁄₁₆ in. (2mm) drill bit, make holes halfway through the legs at the positions marked by arrows on the templates, at right angles to the previous holes.

6 Glue the two chair sections together with the remaining struts and back slats in position. Finish with varnish. Make a woven seat using a single color thread and following the instructions for the Shaker chair on page 58. Instructions for a cushion to complete the chair are given on page 27.

PAINTED CEILING

An elegant ceiling is a striking feature of this interior—decorative and attractive, yet not ostentatious. The designs are created with just four colors of paint on a brown background giving a *trompe l'oeil* (meaning fooling the eye) effect of three-dimensional leaves and ornate architectural curls.

1 Cut a piece of board to fit the ceiling, and paint with matte brown latex paint. Cut strips of thick cardboard to make a border around the ceiling edge, and a large circle in the middle of the ceiling. Seal with acrylic varnish, then paint the strips with gold acrylic paint.

2 Using the photograph as a guide, paint in the outlines of curls and leaves using ochre paint. Emphasize the shadows of the design with dark brown paint. Work some leaves in white, with gray shadows to make them appear three-dimensional.

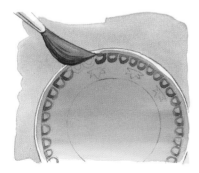

3 Paint the circular rosette panel in red. Add regular geometric details around the edge in dark brown. Glue the golden strips and rosette border to the brown cardboard.

4 Using dark brown paint and a fine brush, paint in floral and leaf flourishes at the corners and joins of the strips. When complete, secure the finished ceiling piece to the ceiling with PVA wood glue.

GOLDEN WALL PANEL

Repeated across the back wall of the room, and framed with strips of wood with mitered corners, these painted panels are a lavish addition to a lying-in room. The panels have a rich golden background—the perfect setting for painted scenes of birds and trees.

1 Cut a rectangle of cardboard and paint it with gold acrylic paint.

2 With brown acrylic paint and a fine brush, paint in the lines of branches and twigs crossing the panel. With dark green acrylic paint, add leaves and curling tendrils to the branches.

3 Cut tiny pictures of birds from a greeting card catalog or wildlife magazine. Glue them to the panel. Alternatively, paint stylized birds with a few strokes of paint. Frame the panel with strips of flat molding, glued to the edges of the cardboard. Tape several panels to the wall to finalize the arrangement, and then glue them in place.

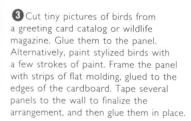

EMBELLISH A DOOR

Painted scenes such as these can also be used to embellish a paneled door. Cut card to fit door panels, decorate, then glue in position. Lines of narrow molding can be used to finish the edges, cut into miters at each corner.

PERIOD POINTS

• The projects in this chapter utilize basic techniques and materials to help you recreate the refined setting of a 17-century lying-in room, an essential dollhouse feature of this period.

• Choose luxurious silk fabrics and satin ribbons to swathe around the bed and cot to emphasize these items as focal points of the room. Offset this luxury with plain wooden furniture and practical wicker-work baskets.

• A few carefully chosen period pictures, depicting family life and agricultural scenes, can be chosen as soothing themes, to interest the new mother in her period of lying in. Furnished with ornate, yet not ostentatious, gilded frames, they are the perfect period details to complete your room.

18th-Century Merchant's
silver room

Use ready-made architectural dollhouse flourishes to embellish ornate wall brackets.

Dollhouses of the eighteenth century are masterpieces of craftsmanship created using the very finest skills and materials. This elegant mid-eighteenth-century merchant's room is from a Dutch cabinet dollhouse that was put together by a remarkable dollhouse enthusiast called Sara Ploos van Amstel. Cabinet dollhouses were rarely designed as playthings, but were often the hobby of wealthy women. This room was created to display Sara Ploos van Amstel's collection of miniature silver, for which she had a special love. Such display rooms might also contain collections of Dutch or Chinese blue and white porcelain. Whilst sparsely furnished, the individual pieces in this room are of very good quality—walnut chairs and a pedestal table with a cherry-twist support and an embroidered top, stitched by Sara Ploos van Amstel herself.

The style of the room is a mixture of Palladian and Rococo elements—both popular styles in the mid-eighteenth century. Classical Palladian columns, shell motifs and decorative supports lend a dignified elegance to the room, whereas gold Rococo flourishes reflect an air of self-indulgence and the love of fine things. In this chapter, you can learn how to choose the materials and objects to create a fine eighteenth-century display room.

Typically, carpets in eighteenth-century dollhouses were painted directly onto the floor, like this fine example with Turkish patterns.

THE BASICS

◀ MAKING A FLOOR
The rich hues and patterns of a Turkish carpet have been painted directly onto a board that lines the floor of this wealthy merchant's room—a popular technique for miniature floor coverings in the eighteenth and nineteenth centuries. Use the directions on page 35 to plan your own painted carpet, using just four colors of acrylic paint.

◀ THE WALLS
An important principle of eighteenth-century interior design is demonstrated in the walls of this room: a harmonious balance of crimson red, white and gold make a rich and slightly ostentatious background against which items valued by the household can be displayed. Curls, flourishes, and gilded patterning are all carefully controlled in designs based on natural forms and are used to frame or support oil paintings and fine silver items.

▶ CEILING
In classical Rococo style, no surface remains undecorated. Complementing the painted floor, a skyscape has been painted onto the ceiling, indicating that the family is rich enough to hire the services of a fine artist. To recreate this ceiling effect, cut a scene from a greetings card or art catalog. Skyscapes and scenes incorporating angels and cherubs are suitable. Cut a frame from thin brown cardboard, painted with lines of ochre and dark brown paint to give a three-dimensional effect. Glue it to the ceiling, framing the painted scene.

FURNITURE AND FITTINGS

▶ CHAIR

Sturdy and comfortable walnut chairs in Queen Anne style reveal that despite the ornate fittings and golden decorations, this room has practical uses. It is the setting for the merchant's meetings and informal receptions — designed to impress clients and make them comfortable, easing the business negotiations. The set of four chairs has fine-quality walnut backs, a touch of carving on the legs, and green velvet seats. See page 34 for instructions.

▼ PICTURE

Respect for status, hierarchy, and economic power was important to the occupants of this household. Portraits of royalty and historical figures quietly observe all the dealings that take place in the room. The portraits are given stately elegance with ornate golden frames. These miniature frames can be recreated with polymer clay built on a cardboard base. Sprayed gold, they take on the look of carved and gilded wood.

▲ VALANCE BOARD AND COLUMNS

Strong lines of white paneling and pillars frame the crimson walls, giving a striking and decorative style to the room. Make panels from strips of wood, sand, and color with white latex paint. Cut curved valance boards from cardboard and color with the same paint. Embellish the pieces with red leaves and flourishes. These surface decorations can then be enlivened with touches of gold metallic paint applied with a fine paintbrush.

WALL PANEL

The walls in this cabinet house have been lined with crimson silk. Good-quality crimson cardboard can also be used to line the walls to give the impression of smooth painted plaster. Whatever the material, a strong color will give real character and unity to the room, contrasting with the white paneling and gold-painted details.

◀ PEDESTAL TABLE

An octagonal pedestal table provides just enough surface to carry a teapot and tea strainer to welcome guests with a hot drink. Designed as a card games table, three legs in a "tripod" form give the table stability, and a cherry-twist support shows the craftsmanship with which this table has been constructed. Follow the instructions on page 35 to make a pedestal table for your own dollhouse room.

▶ SIDE TABLE

Cherry-twist legs are also a feature of the elegant side table. Choose a table in a dark wood such as walnut or teak, with an attractively grained top. A varnished surface will show off a display of silver to its best advantage.

DISPLAY ALCOVE

The centerpiece of the room, the display alcove illustrates the eighteenth-century love of ornate decoration and fine craftsmanship. The display can be created by building it up from separate ornamental shapes, painted in gold and white and used as components of the finished design.

▲ DRAPES

Above the display alcove, a swagged drape of red velvet completes the top of the display with a hint of luxury. A rectangle of soft red velour fabric, edged with gold braid or fringe, can be attached to the inside of the alcove frame, and then gathered up and tied in the center with thread. Add tiny gold tassels, available from haberdashery shops.

ADD TO THE LOOK

▶ MIRROR

Used to add a lightness and elegance to the room, mirrors reflect light from the silver items on display. Some rooms of this period, especially function rooms, were lined with mirrors with exaggerated, ornate frames. This was especially popular for ballrooms, so that the guests could see themselves as they danced in the beautiful surroundings. This mirror, designed to be displayed above a fireplace, has been framed with strips of wooden dowel and shaped wood strip, colored with gold metallic paint. A single scallop shell (made from a shaped button, painted gold) at the top of the frame is a symbol of the Roman goddess Venus, born of the sea.

Fine silver forms an important part of a wealthy eighteenth-century scene. Tiny silverware is very popular with dollhouse enthusiasts, as the items demonstrate the skill of the silversmith. Inexpensive additions can be created by coloring miniature plastic goblets and plates with silver paint. Alternatively, use the display shelves to hold a collection of blue and white Dutch or Chinese porcelain, or china figurines, which were all popular items in the eighteenth century.

CHAIR

These formal chairs in Queen Anne style are robust and well made, with just a touch of carving at the tops of the legs to ensure that they harmonize with their decorative surroundings. The woodwork is smooth and the chairs have no arms, making them suitable for elegant eighteenth-century ladies wearing voluminous dresses to sit in comfort. Choose an attractive fine-grain wood such as walnut for an authentic finish for these elegant pieces of furniture.

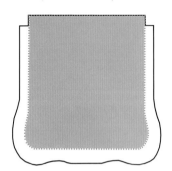

padded seat template

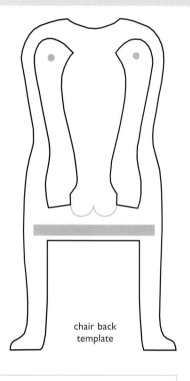

chair back template

1 Copy the chair back template onto paper and cut it out. Draw round the template on ⅗₆ in. (5mm) thick wood. Drill two holes in the positions marked by gray dots on the diagram, large enough for a coping-saw blade. With a small chisel, cut a ⅛ in. (3mm) deep slot, marked in gray on the template.

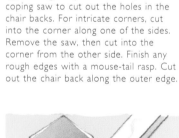

2 Holding the piece in a vise, use a coping saw to cut out the holes in the chair backs. For intricate corners, cut into the corner along one of the sides. Remove the saw, then cut into the corner from the other side. Finish any rough edges with a mouse-tail rasp. Cut out the chair back along the outer edge.

3 With a knife, mark two lines on the chair back as stop cuts. Use a flat chisel to shave a little wood away up to the cut line. Sand all the cut edges of the chair back.

TIP

It is quite tricky to get two carved legs to match up. If you are making more than one chair, make all of the front legs and choose matching pairs when they are all finished.

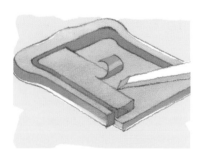

4 Copy the seat template onto paper. Cut it out and draw around it on ⅜ in. (8mm) thick wood. Using a coping saw, cut out the shape and sand all cut edges. Use a craft knife to outline the shape marked in gray on the template. This is a stop cut. Use a flat chisel to remove a layer of ⅛ in. (3mm) thick from the shaded area up to the line of the cut.

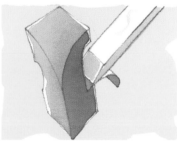

5 Cut two ready-made chair legs to 1³⁄₁₆ in. (30mm) long, or if you prefer to carve them yourself, cut two 2⅜ in. (60mm) long sections from ⅜ in. (10mm) square wood strip. Hold one piece in a vise. Shape the top with a chisel, then carve away the lower area, making a curve to the foot. The shaped piece should be 1³⁄₁₆ in. (30mm) long. Sand, then cut the leg from the large block.

6 Stain all of the pieces. Assemble and glue the chair together as shown in the diagram. Finish with gloss varnish.

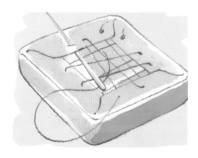

7 Using only the gray area of the padded seat template, cut one piece of thick cardboard and one piece of ¼ in. (6mm) thick foam. Cut a piece of velvet ⅝ in. (16mm) bigger than the padded seat template all round. Use a needle and thread to lace the velvet over the foam and onto the cardboard. Trim off excess fabric and glue the seat into the seat recess on the chair.

PEDESTAL TABLE

A pedestal table is light enough to move around the room, allowing it to be positioned by the fire in winter, or by the window on a sunny day. Designed as a card table, the fine floral embroidery on its fabric surface provides an interesting talking point. As a tea table, the embroidery is protected from drips by a saucer on which to store the silver tea strainer.

pedestal table leg template

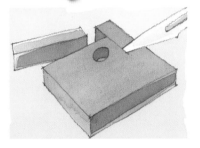

1 Copy the leg template onto paper and cut it out. From ⅛ in. (3mm) thick wood, cut three legs and one piece 2⅛ in. (54mm) square. Cut the corners from the square to create an octagon. With a 3⁄16 in. (5mm) drill bit, drill a hole in a piece of 3⁄16 in. (5mm) thick wood, then cut out a square around the hole to give a square with edges of about ⅜ in. (10mm). This is the support block. Sand and stain all of the pieces.

2 From 3⁄16 in. (5mm) diameter ready-made cherry-twist wood (available from specialist dollhouse suppliers), cut a 1⅝ in. (41mm) long pole. Stain to match the other pieces. Glue the end into the support block. Trim a little wood from three sides of the end of the pole to give flat surfaces against which to glue the legs.

3 Glue a 2⅜ in. (60mm) diameter octagon of embroidered or textured fabric onto the surface of the table, folding and gluing the edges onto the edge of the table. Cut Vs into the fabric at each corner to help the fabric lie neatly. Finish with a strip of braid around the table edge.

4 Assemble and glue the table as shown in the diagram, using fast-drying contact adhesive. Varnish to finish.

PAINTED TURKISH CARPET

Just four paint colors, carefully planned, are used to create the stylized plant and floral motifs so characteristic of Turkish rugs and carpets in the eighteenth century. Use slightly textured cardboard, acrylic paints, and a fine paintbrush.

1 Cut a piece of board the same size as your room, paint with black acrylic, and leave to dry. Using the picture above as a guide, copy the carpet pattern onto paper slightly smaller than the board.

2 Tape the paper on top of the black board. With a hard pencil, draw over the design, pressing down into the board to leave an impression, and then remove the paper.

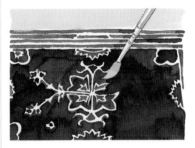

3 Using the pencil impressions as a guide, mark the lightest details in ochre paint, then leave to dry. Add further areas in gray.

4 With red paint, add the final areas. When dry, varnish the whole board. Use an oil-based varnish so that the paint will not smudge.

WALLS AND PANELING

The walls of this room are lined with crimson moiré silk fabric. This can be very difficult to control. For the best result, cover thick cardboard with spray glue and smooth the silk over the top. Leave to dry thoroughly, then use the following instructions to cut cardboard to line the walls. Ensure the edges are covered by molding and paneling to avoid the silk fraying. Alternatively, recreate painted plaster with plain painted cardboard, as shown in the picture.

panel frame templates

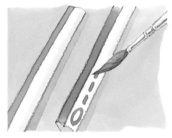

❶ Cut pieces of thick, colored cardboard (or silk-covered cardboard) to fit each section of wall. Where they meet shaped edges—such as around the fireplace and beside the door—use a craft knife to shape the cardboard before gluing in place.

❷ Color strips of beading with white latex paint. Add a stripe of crimson acrylic paint and oval shapes at regular intervals. Finish with details picked out in gold metallic paint. Cut strips to fit around the base and tops of the walls, with mitered corners to fit neatly together. Glue them in place.

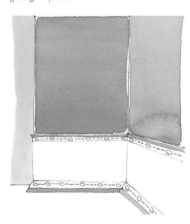

❸ Cut 1½ in. (38mm) strips of thick white cardboard as paneling and glue them above the lower beading. Make and fit strips of painted beading just above the paneling.

❹ Cut a 2¼ in. (5mm) x 1 in. (25mm) rectangle of white paper for each wall section. Paint decorative swags in red paint, copying the picture. Using the panel frame templates, cut two frames of red paper and glue them to the panel. Pick out details in the frames and swags using gold metallic paint. Glue the decorative panels to the white cardboard on the walls.

ORNATE PICTURE FRAME

❶ Copy the oval picture frame template onto paper and cut it out. Draw round it on thick cardboard and cut it out. Place the frame over a picture from a greetings card or magazine. Draw round the outer edge and cut it out.

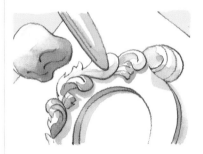

❷ Place the cardboard frame on a spare scrap of cardboard. Use polymer clay to build up the shapes and curls of the picture frame, piece by piece, on top of the frame. Use a blunt stick to make textures in the clay, and to smooth the edges of the pieces into each other.

❸ When complete, bake to harden, following the manufacturer's instructions. You can bake the whole piece on the cardboard, as the oven will not get hot enough to burn it. When cool, glue the clay to the cardboard frame and color the whole piece with gold metallic spray.

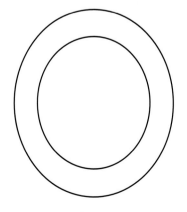

picture frame template

❹ Glue the portrait on the back, then tape on a hanging thread of fine gold cord, tied in a bow at the top.

SILVER DISPLAY UNIT

Plastic flourishes to
embellish the wall brackets

The chief feature of the room, the display alcove, gives special prominence to the pieces of silver and porcelain displayed there. Such was the fascination for ornate decoration in the eighteenth century that it gave rise to a whole language describing symbolic shapes and flourishes. The brackets holding up the items in the densely clustered display illustrate some of the popular shapes of the period, with names such as "anthemion": A shape based on the honeysuckle flower; "palmette": A fan of palm leaves; "volutes": Carefully crafted spiral scrolls—such as those on the legs supporting the low shelf at the base of the display; "acanthus": Stylized leaves of the

acanthus plant—often carved at the top of pillars; and "lambrequins": Motifs representing tasseled cloth.

Cast-plaster supports and plastic flourishes and edgings are available from dollhouse suppliers and model shops. Plastic pieces can be used whole, or cut up to provide swirls and leafy edging to build up the design. Once colored with white and gold paints, these separate pieces become harmonized into a single design. Shelves can be created with semicircles of wood held up by a triangular bracket, painted gold, or by gluing a semicircle to the top of a plastic bracket. Edging pieces can also be created, especially for a low shelf at the bottom of the display, from shaped white paper, decorated with gold paint.

Plastic, plaster,
and wooden
supports

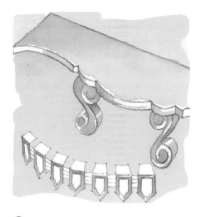

❶ Cut a piece of thick white cardboard to fit the alcove or panel where you will place your display. Start to plan your layout by placing some ready-made plaster or wooden brackets onto the cardboard. From plastic pieces sold as architectural dollhouse flourishes, cut decorative pieces to join up the design. Frames for special pieces such as silver platters can be shaped from polymer clay, following the instructions for the molded picture frame on page 36.

❷ When the layout is complete, remove the pieces and paint them with white enamel paint. When dry, pick out details in gold metallic paint. Reassemble the display and glue the pieces to the cardboard, then glue the whole piece into the alcove or onto the wall panel.

❸ From ⅛ in. (3mm) thick wood, cut a shelf shape to fit across the alcove, painted white with a gold edge. Glue the edge to the wall. Cut and paint curled pieces from the plastic architectural flourishes, to glue in place as supports.

❹ Using the template, cut a shaped decorative edge from thin white cardboard. Highlight the edges with gold paint. Fold the tabs along the dotted lines marked on the template, and glue them under the edge of the shelf.

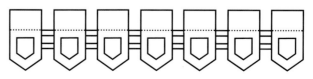

shelf edge template

PERIOD POINTS

• The projects in this chapter are designed to capture an 18th-century style that is both wealthy and extravagant, with splendid items such as gilded picture frames, embellished wall panels, and a decorative mirror above the fireplace.

• Display a collection of beautiful silverware or delicate miniature porcelain in a specially designed alcove set into the wall. Create ornate brackets and shelves from ready-made cast plaster supports and tie them into a unified design with dollhouse architectural flourishes.

• Create an authentic 18th-century dollhouse floor covering by painting exotic Turkish designs onto a prepared board and fitting it into your dollhouse room.

Colonial
dining room

The colonial style was prominent in America from about 1730 to 1790. It blended American elements with classical aspects of contemporary British design imported to America in pattern books, illustrations, and engravings that were pored over by enthusiastic householders. Grand colonial houses are associated with the emergence of a wealthy middle class in the eastern states of America. They were built upon sound structural and social principles—the most common feature being a large central hall from which spacious reception rooms opened up on either side. This layout lent itself to relaxed social gatherings at which guests felt free to wander in and out of different rooms and to drift in and out of conversations and activities. Unmistakable features of this style and period of architecture include a love of symmetry and classical design expressed in statuesque porticos and archways, glass fanlights, large symmetrical staircases, high ceilings, wooden flooring, and marble fireplaces. In this chapter, you will learn how to re-create many of the characteristic features of a dining room in a grand eighteenth-century American colonial home.

With its exquisite cut lattice, this jade-effect table is typical of the fine craftsmanship of the period.

THE BASICS

MAKING A FLOOR
A pattern of parquet tiles combines light and dark woods to give a pleasing effect across large areas of open floor. This can be achieved by gluing wood tiles in a pattern on to the dollhouse floor, or you can line the floor with parquet-effect paper. Across the doorways, add a strip of ⅟₁₆ in. (2mm) thick plain polished wood.

▼ COVING
Smooth, cream walls are topped by a line of shaped coving with a castellated pattern at the base. Coving in this style is available from dollhouse suppliers. Alternatively, adapt plain, curved coving. Using a craft knife, make a series of regular nicks along the bottom edge of the coving, and then remove every other square to give the characteristic pattern. Instructions for making paneling and using plain and shaped coving are on page 44.

▶ DOOR
At the top of a flight of marble steps on the outside of the building, guests were welcomed through a large solid wooden door into the house. They were then led into a grand open hallway with an impressive staircase and archways opening on either side. Everything was designed to give a sense of spaciousness and light.

FURNITURE AND FITTINGS

◀EMBROIDERED DRAPES

Crewelwork embroidery was a popular pastime for young women of the colonial period, and was considered a proper and ladylike pursuit. Often worked in woolen yarn on a coarse-weave fabric, the designs were based on natural themes, such as flowers or birds. Many colors were incorporated, making the work spirited and attractive, and bringing a lively tone to the room. Instructions for making the drapes are on page 43.

▲ JADE TABLE

The love of exquisite items from the Far East demonstrates the colonial connection with craftspeople in many continents. Fretwork on the side panels of this little side table carry motifs of stylized curls and bars, emblems of the fine carving on many oriental items of the period. This dollhouse table is made from cardboard mottled with yellow-green paint to mimic jade—a much prized and beautiful stone. Instructions for making a jade-effect table are on page 45.

◀URNS

Two classic urns, with a dark green glaze and gilded rims and handles, grace the mantelpiece. Based on an ancient Roman design, they show the family's love of fine ornaments and craftsmanship.

◀FIREPLACE

A grand fireplace is a prominent feature of this stately room. Plasterwork surrounds are available from many dollhouse suppliers; models with a black marble surround are particularly suitable. A lining of brick paper can be added for an authentic finish. Polished brass fittings will also add to the effect, with a low rail surrounding the fire and bright fire irons.

▶MILITARY PORTRAIT

Above the fireplace, a magnificent portrait is prominently displayed, demonstrating the household's admiration for military and naval heroes. Fine gilded frames can be created from lengths of wooden molding, painted with gold metallic paint and embellished with motifs cut from artificial foliage. Instructions are on page 44.

◀CHAIRS

A set of ornate chairs with an accompanying dining table make a beautiful centerpiece to this room, set on an embroidered rug. Each chair has a distinctively detailed fretwork shield for a back piece and a rich embroidered cushion featuring a stitched pattern of leaves and flowers. Choose floss colors and flower shapes to match elements in the curtains and rug. The chair covers can also be created from ready-embroidered dressmaking ribbon or brocade.

◀SILVER CANDLESTICKS

In the eighteenth century, candles were the main source of light for the family. Chandeliers in each function room provided the main illumination, but individual candlesticks were also important to give atmospheric lighting. They would also have been used by guests wishing to find their way to their bedrooms in unfamiliar surroundings.

▶SIDEBOARD

This pretty little sideboard would have stored glassware, napkins, cutlery, and other dining accessories ready for evenings of entertainment. With elegantly tapering legs and a fine polished surface, this type of furniture would have been made from a tropical wood, such as mahogany or teak. Instructions for making a similar sideboard are on page 42.

ADD TO THE LOOK

CHANDELIER

A brass chandelier carrying ten tall candles provides the main source of light in this large room. Hung from a sturdy yet decorative chain, it would be lowered at the end of the evening for servants to trim the wicks, replace spent candles, and remove any spilled wax. Position a chandelier in the very center of the ceiling. If you wish, add a simple decorative plaster rose on the ceiling to surround the chain.

A display of beautiful jade items or silverware is an appropriately showy addition to this colonial dining room, demonstrating the family's wealth and love of fine art and crafts. Select a few colorful items for the mantelpiece and a set of silverware to go on the sideboard, and then place them in an attractive arrangement to show them off to their best advantage.

SIDEBOARD

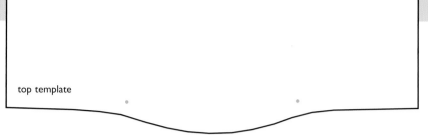

Angled doors and a bow-fronted drawer are handsome features of this decorative and functional sideboard. As a store for domestic items such as cutlery and glassware—the sideboard kept useful items close at hand for busy serving staff. It has a polished surface on which to display a collection of fine silverware. The following instructions are for a similar sideboard of the colonial period.

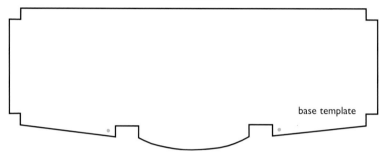

top template

base template

❶ From ⅛ in. (3mm) thick wood, cut the following:
Sides: 2 pieces, each 1 × 1½ in. (25 × 38mm)
Supports: 2 pieces, each 1 × ⅛ in. (25 × 3mm)
Doors: 2 pieces, each 1¹⁄₁₆ × 1¼ in. (27 × 32mm)
Back: 1 piece, 3¾ × 1¼ in. (95 × 32mm)
Front panel: 1 piece, 1³⁄₁₆ × 1¼ in. (30 × 32mm)
Copy the base and top templates onto paper and cut them out. Draw round them on ⅛ in. (3mm) thick wood and cut them out.
Lightly sand and stain all of the pieces.

❷ From ¼ in. (6mm) square wood, cut six legs, each 2¾ in. (70mm) long. Use a sharp knife to taper the end of each leg slightly. Sand and stain.

❸ Glue each side panel between a pair of legs and clamp together until dry. Glue the supports along the inside bottom edge of each side panel.

❹ With a ¹⁄₃₂ in. (1mm) drill bit, make holes in the positions marked in gray on the base and top templates.

❺ Glue the remaining two legs into the slots at the front of the base piece and the back piece along the back edge of the base. Glue the side panels in place.

❻ From ⅜ in. (10mm) thick wood, cut a drawer front, ⅜ × 1 ¹⁄₁₆ in. (10 × 27mm). With a knife, trim it into a curved shape. Sand and stain, then glue to the front panel of the sideboard. Varnish all of the sideboard pieces.

❼ With a ¹⁄₃₂ in. (1mm) drill bit, make a hinge hole in the top and bottom corner of each door. Push pins through the holes in the base and up into the corners of the doors. Trim and sand the doors to help them fit in position.

❽ Glue the top to the sideboard, making sure not to get glue on the door areas. Push pins down through the holes in the top into the tops of the doors. When dry, sand smooth. Add small wooden beads as drawer and door handles.

DOOR

Broad lines of paneling lend solidity and grandeur to a plain wooden door. These can be added to a ready-made door as strips of thick cardboard, then painted to give the impression of a single shaped piece. Top the door with a fanlight of radiating fretwork lines—a classic feature for this period of house.

EMBROIDERED DRAPES

Textiles were an important feature of colonial interiors. Expensive silks, silk damasks, embroidered fabrics, and brocade, imported from India and the Orient, were evident in fashionable households. These embroidered crewelwork drapes illustrate motifs popular in the colonial period—stylized flowers, leaves, and vines picked out in green, pink, and yellow on a white background.

❶ Remove the door handle from the existing door and sand the door to roughen the surface. Close the door and draw a pencil line around the edge, where the door butts up to the frame.

❷ Cut ½ in. (12mm) wide strips of ¹⁄₁₆ in. (2mm) thick cardboard. Glue three, equally spaced strips in vertical lines on the door, keeping inside the pencil marks.

❶ Cut two pieces of thin white cotton (lawn cotton is suitable), each 2 in. (50mm) taller than your dollhouse windows, and about three-quarters of the width of the whole window area, plus 1 in. (25mm).

❷ With green embroidery floss and overlapping straight stitches, work several curved vine shapes, evenly spaced across each drape. With pink embroidery floss, use small overlapping stitches to outline a few flowers and buds.

❸ Cut short pieces of ½ in. (12mm) wide strips of cardboard and glue them between the uprights.

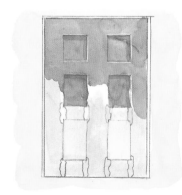

❹ Fill the cracks between the cardboard pieces with plastic wood or other filling agent. When dry, sand smooth and paint the door with brown acrylic paint. Varnish to finish, then refit the door handle.

❸ With yellow embroidery floss, make a few overlapping stitches at the center of each flower.

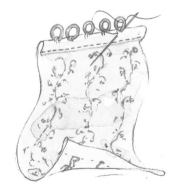

❹ Use white thread to hem the drapes around the edges. Sew tiny brass rings, equally spaced, along the top edge of the drapes. These can be used to hang them from a curtain pole.

PORTRAITS

The family of a colonial household would be very proud of its military past, and revered those who had served their country in conquering new regions and establishing trading links around the world. Large oil paintings of eminent military heroes were therefore an important feature of a colonial household, representing links with the past and inspiration for the future.

ADAPTING A PHOTOGRAPH

If you have access to a scanner and a computer with image-manipulation software, you can adapt a family photograph to look like an oil painting. Print off the finished picture in color, and frame using the techniques described here.

FINDING PICTURES

Reproductions of oil paintings are a popular subject for greeting cards and appear in art and greeting card catalogs. Cut out the pictures and mount them on cardboard before framing as described here.

1 Cut a military portrait from an art catalog or greeting card and glue it to a rectangle of cardboard leaving a ¼ in. (6mm) border.

2 For a simple frame, cut lengths of wooden molding with mitered corners. Paint the pieces with gold metallic paint and glue them around the portrait.

3 For an ornate frame, frame the portrait with wooden molding as in step 2. Cut ornate flourishes from thin cardboard, or use leaf shapes cut from artificial plants, and glue to the corners and edges of the frame. Paint gold.

WALL PANELING AND COVING

Tall walls and high ceilings were a common feature of colonial interiors. Carefully selected paneling and coving give the room a cool elegance. Recreate this effect in your own dollhouse room using thick cardboard for paneling and strips of molded wood for the skirting board, chair rail, and coving.

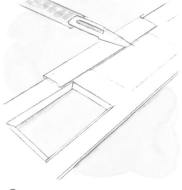

1 Paint the wall with pale cream acrylic paint. Cut 3 in. (75mm) wide strips of ¹⁄₁₆ in. (2mm) thick cardboard to run around the bottom of the walls. In each strip, use a craft knife and metal ruler to cut out rectangles at regular intervals, each approximately 1³⁄₁₆ × 2³⁄₈ in. (30 x 60mm). Hold the knife at an angle to give cuts that slope inwards.

2 Glue the cardboard strips to the wall. From shaped wooden molding, cut the skirting board for the bottom and a chair rail for the top of the paneling. Paint the molding and wall paneling with dark cream acrylic paint, then glue the skirting board and chair rail in place.

3 Cut lengths of shaped coving to fit around the top of the walls. Paint to match the paneling, then glue in place.

JADE-EFFECT TABLE

This dollhouse table is made from white cardboard that was stippled with yellow-green paint to give the impression of jade. A remarkably resilient stone, jade could be carved into fine detail but was also used to form strong structural items. Jade has been used by artists, especially in China, for thousands of years and is prized for its translucent beauty when shaped and polished. This jade-effect table is an unusual piece for a dollhouse room. Nothing like it would usually be found in a human-scale room, as jade is so rare and sought-after that a whole table would be a prohibitively expensive piece. In miniature, this jade-effect table is a fine addition to a colonial dining room.

table base template

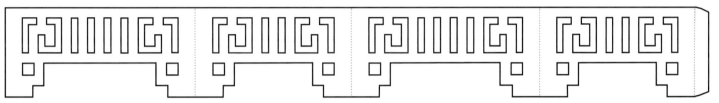

1 Copy the table base template onto paper, and then glue the strip onto white cardboard. Using a flat-ended brush (a stippling brush), dab yellow-green paint in a mottled pattern across the whole surface of the cardboard. Repeat on the other side.

2 Use a craft knife to cut out the fine fretwork design. Score the cardboard along the dotted lines marked in gray on the template.

3 Fold the base piece along the scored lines, and then glue the tab in place to hold the base in a rectangle.

4 Paint two rectangles of $\frac{1}{16}$ in. (2mm) thick white cardboard: one lower piece $1\frac{13}{16}$ x $2\frac{1}{4}$ in. (46 x 56mm), and one upper piece 2 x $2\frac{3}{8}$ in. (50 x 60mm). Glue the pieces together, and then glue them to the top of the table. Stipple with green paint.

CREATIVE PAINT EFFECTS

The decorative lattice sides of this table would make it an attractive addition to other periods of dollhouse. If a jade finish is not to your taste, the paint effect can easily be varied to suit your chosen period style or color scheme. Black painted sides could be finished with a top covered with marbled paper. For a modern Chinese look, paint the sides red and the top black, finished with gloss varnish. The finished table could even be painted all over with silver metallic paint for a modern chrome look, mixing contemporary style with classic oriental patterns.

PERIOD POINTS

• Plan your colonial house with a layout centered upon a large entrance hall. Create rooms that open up on either side through wide, graceful arches for an open and welcoming feel.

• Choose furniture and fittings that reflect the wealth and refinement of the family, with beautiful ornaments made from jade and silver, and fine porcelain to grace the mantelpiece.

• A colonial family's attachment to history calls for the addition of impressive military and naval portraits to this dining room.

• A set of elegant chairs and a highly polished dining table are shown off to their best advantage when set upon a top quality embroidered rug in pretty shades of pinks and greens.

Chinoiserie
sitting room

This table was designed to display precious ornaments.

With the rapid expansion of travel and trade, mid-eighteenth century British adventurers brought home many fabulous works of art from the Far East. Such was the fascination with tales of distant lands that it was not long before oriental designs were incorporated into the interior design of fashionable homes in a period style called chinoiserie. Ornate gilding and fretwork designs fitted well with the rococo style—graceful designs using motifs such as shells and scrolls—that was also popular at the time, and Eastern designs were quickly adopted by furniture makers and craftsmen. This scene, a replica of a room at England's Windsor Castle, shows how furniture designs common in the eighteenth century were decorated to reflect chinoiserie style. It is interesting to note that despite their fascination with exotic Eastern design, many people made no distinction between the many cultures they were drawn from. Often Chinese, Japanese, and other Asian motifs were displayed in one room. Symbols—such as painted peacocks, pagodas, and wise old men—were used to denote a general exotic or oriental feel.

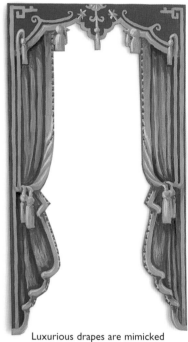

Luxurious drapes are mimicked with a clever paint technique.

THE BASICS

▼ MAKING A FLOOR
A simple, smooth floor covering in a neutral color makes a good background against which to display the striking shapes of the black and gold lacquer-work furniture. Fabrics such as felt and fine baize are suitable, as well as smooth brushed cotton or cotton velvet. Avoid synthetic or bright colors and artificial fibers with a modern sheen.

◀ WINDOW FRAMES
A simple frame of cream-colored cardboard, outlined with sepia frame lines, gives the effect of elegant eighteenth-century windows. Set back from the main walls, the window alcove provides space for a small table where the occupant of the room could sit to write letters, with a good view of the stately garden outside.

◀ THE WALLS
This whole room has been lined with fine-quality, cream watercolor paper, with features drawn on in sepia-colored ink. Complex oriental fretwork patterns at the corners and base of each wall panel make frames for painted Chinese scrolls. A layout guide for one of these ornate panels is included on page 52.

FURNITURE AND FITTINGS

▼CHAIRS
These stately chairs are intended for the formal surroundings of a sitting room, where guests might engage in polite conversation. Clothing in the mid-eighteenth century tended to restrict movement, so chairs were designed to enable sitters to maintain an elegant upright posture, from which they were free to make courteous hand gestures to emphasize their speech. Instructions for making the chairs are on page 50.

▶ORNATE DISPLAY STAND
A model of a Chinese man with a straw hat and embroidered robe is displayed in a special Chinese stand, embellished with brass bells and a red lacquer top. Bells and pagoda roof shapes incorporated into decorative furniture design were popular chinoiserie motifs.

▼CHAISE LONGUE
The graceful curves of the chaise longue offer a comfortable place for the lady of the house to rest, put her feet up and enjoy a cup of tea, delivered to her side by her servant. Assembled from flat wooden pieces, this replica of an eighteenth-century chaise longue has been japanned—painted in black to imitate Chinese lacquerwork—then embellished with geometric designs and flourishes worked in gold paint. Directions for making this fine piece of furniture can be found on page 51.

▶PAGODA
Many of the objects in this room are decorated with pagoda motifs—a favorite symbol of Eastern style. They are used on the lacquer-work furniture: The motif is painted in miniature on the flat panels on the backs of the chairs, and on the side of the wooden cabinet it is surrounded by elegant fronds of bamboo. These pagoda ornaments are created from polymer modeling clay, baked to harden then finished with painted details.

▼STOOL
This stool is based on a classic shape from the eighteenth century, inspired by an ancient Roman design for a low-level bench. Topped by a flat cushion in textured silk, it makes a comfortable seat for someone wishing to speak casually with the person on the chaise longue, or an informal seat for a child.

▼CABINET
Formal occasions—such as a visit from friends or neighbors—meant that the room had to be cleared of everyday clutter so that guests might receive a simple and refined welcome. A large cabinet might hold fine linen tablecloths to adorn a table setting for afternoon tea. Boxes might also be stored there containing embroidery belonging to the lady of the house. This cabinet has an attractive finish, having been rubbed down to reveal areas of a red paint undercoat, to give an authentic lacquer-work finish. The instructions are on page 52.

▶DISPLAY TABLE
Ornaments were highly prized, and were often displayed on special pedestal tables shown off to their best advantage in the natural light from a window. With touches of gold paint, pick out special features on the pedestal and legs to create the perfect setting for your oriental objects. Instructions for making this table are on page 50.

▶WALL SCROLL
The scrolls that decorate the walls are classic elements of an interior based on chinoiserie design. Worked on long strips of white watercolor paper, the scrolls carry painted Chinese or Japanese scenes featuring trees, bamboo, deer, peacocks, songbirds, and monkeys. They are painted in characteristic oriental style—a few delicate brushstrokes capturing the grace of natural forms. Instructions for the wall scrolls are on page 52.

ADD TO THE LOOK

▶DECORATIVE COVING
The tops of the walls are finished with strips of stiff, cream watercolor paper decorated with repeat patterns in sepia-colored ink, to give an artistic impression of sculpted plasterwork. Layout guides for each of the patterns are given on page 53. The patterns can also be used to frame a doorway or give an ornate edging to a window frame.

Ornaments, figurines and fine porcelain are all suitable items for display in this Chinese room. The blue and white box on the side table is a tiny porcelain pillbox. The figurine on the right of the picture stands on top of a tall wooden dollhouse vase. Cover the top with a small circle of cardboard, and glue three small beads to the base as feet. Paint the stand black to look like lacquer, and then decorate with touches of gold paint.

 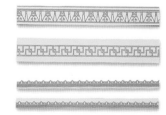  

CHAIR

The two types of chair in this scene are created with the same basic pattern, with the addition of elegantly curved arms to create a formal armchair for an especially honored guest. The shapes are cut from wood, and then painted black to mimic lacquerwork popular in chinoiserie design. Add delicate markings and decorations in gold paint for a stylish finish.

❶ Copy the chair templates onto paper and cut them out. Draw round the templates as follows:
Sides: two pieces, on ³⁄₁₆ in. (5mm) thick wood
Seat: one piece, on ³⁄₁₆ in. (5mm) thick wood
Shaped back bar: one piece, on ¹⁄₁₆ in. (2mm) thick wood
Square back bar: one piece, on ¹⁄₁₆ in. (2mm) thick wood
For an armchair: two arm pieces from ³⁄₁₆ in. (5mm) thick wood. Note: If you are making an armchair, use sandpaper to remove the lower part of the handle curve up to the dotted line marked on the template.

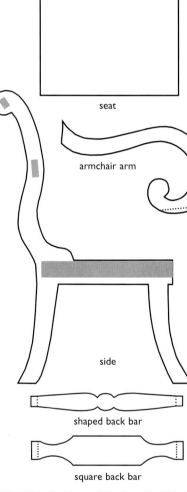

seat

armchair arm

side

shaped back bar

square back bar

❷ Using a coping saw, cut out the pieces. Cut into the corner along one of the sides. Remove the saw and then cut into the corner from the other side. Use a mouse-tail rasp to finish rough edges. Sand the cut edges of each piece.

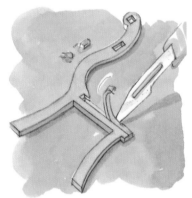

❸ Cut slots into the sidepieces marked in gray on the template to a depth of ¹⁄₁₆ in. (2mm). Cut the slots on the right-hand side of one piece and the left-hand side of the other. Assemble the chair. If you are making an armchair, glue the arm pieces in position.

❹ Paint the chair with black acrylic paint. Use a fine brush and gold metallic paint (acrylic or enamel) to paint designs on the surface. Finish with acrylic varnish. Cut a 2¼ in. (57mm) square of fabric. Fold the edges under to make a 1½ in. (38mm) square. Glue it to the chair seat.

DISPLAY TABLE

Individual conversation pieces— such as a gilded porcelain box or the carved figure of a Japanese warrior—had tables and stands devoted especially to display them. The objects encouraged conversation and were a sign of the house-owner's education and cultured taste in exotic art.

❶ Copy the leg templates onto paper and cut them out. On ¹⁄₁₆ in. (2mm) thick wood, draw round each template three times and use a craft knife to cut out the pieces. From ⅛ in. (3mm) diameter wooden dowel, cut a ⅝ in. (16mm) length. Whittle one end into a point, and cut two shallow notches as shown in the diagram. Finish each table piece with fine-grit paper.

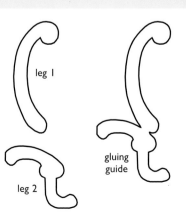

leg 1

leg 2

gluing guide

CHAISE LONGUE

A chaise longue makes an impressive and eye-catching centerpiece for a room, yet it is surprisingly simple to create from just a few cut pieces. Choose a length of fabric with an attractive texture to show off the furniture to its best advantage, and add a bolster and cushion from matching fabric wrapped around pieces of ³⁄₁₆ in. (5mm) thick foam.

① From ³⁄₁₆ in. (5mm) thick wood, cut the following:
Bottom plate: 1¹³⁄₁₆ × 4¹⁵⁄₁₆ in. (46 × 125mm)
Back rest: 1³⁄₁₆ × 1¹³⁄₁₆ in. (30 × 46mm)
From ⅛ in. (3mm) diameter wooden dowel, cut two lengths, each 2 in. (50mm).
From ³⁄₁₆ in. (5mm) thick foam, cut a rectangle 1¹³⁄₁₆ × 4⅝ in. (46 × 117mm).

Copy the chaise longue templates onto paper and cut them out.
Draw round the templates as follows:
Sides: two pieces, on ³⁄₁₆ in. (5mm) thick wood
Bars: two pieces, on ¹⁄₁₆ in. (2mm) thick wood
Legs: four pieces, on ³⁄₁₆ in. (5mm) thick wood

② Using a coping saw, cut out the pieces. For intricate corners, such as under the scrolls, hold the piece in a vise. Use the saw to cut into the corner along one of the sides. Remove the saw and then cut into the corner from the other side. Sand the cut edges of each piece.

③ Cut slots into the side pieces—as marked in gray on the template—to a depth of ¹⁄₁₆ in. (2mm). Make sure that you cut the slots on the right-hand side of one piece and the left-hand side of the other. Assemble the chaise longue as shown in the diagram and glue the pieces together.

④ Paint the chaise longue with black acrylic paint. Use a fine brush and gold metallic paint (acrylic or enamel) to paint designs on the black surface, using the picture as a guide. Finish with acrylic varnish. Glue the foam on top of the bottom plate.

⑤ Cut a rectangle of fabric, 2¾ × 10⅝ in. (70 × 270mm). Fold under ½ in. (12mm) along each long edge and sew it in place. Position the fabric on the chaise longue. Hold it in place at each end of the bottom plate with pins. Trim off the excess fabric at each end, fold under, and use pins to secure it in position.

GOLD PAINTED DETAILS

Gold acrylic or gold metallic enamel paint can be used to add the fine decorative details to black lacquerwork furniture. Enamel paint will give the most luxurious finish.

bar

leg

side

② Place the leg pieces on a flat surface and pair them up, using the gluing guide, *left*. Glue them together, and then leave to dry thoroughly.

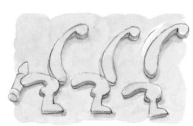

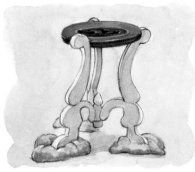

③ Position the leg pieces upright on a flat surface, held in place by reusable putty adhesive, and position the carved dowel in between them. Add a little glue between the pieces and leave to dry. Glue a 1 in. (25mm) diameter wooden button or circle of ¹⁄₁₆ in. (2mm) thick wood to form the top of the table.

④ Paint the table with black acrylic paint. Use a fine brush and gold metallic paint (acrylic or enamel) to paint designs on the black surface. Finish with acrylic varnish. Fill the button holes with airdrying clay. Once dry, paint to match.

CABINET

Beautiful hinges made from etched brass—such as the examples on this chinoiserie cabinet—are available from specialist dollhouse suppliers. With time, the brass will tarnish to give the authentic feel of a treasured family heirloom. If you cannot find hinges to suit your cabinet, you can create your own. Use regular rectangular hinges, then add a decorative shape cut from thin cardboard. Color with brass metallic paint, then glue in place butting up to the hinge. For a decorative lock, look out for a brass-effect jewelry catch with a flat back, to fit to the front of this cabinet's doors.

1 From ⅛ in. (3mm) thick wood, cut the following:
Sides: two pieces, each 1¾ x 3¼ in. (45 x 83mm)
Top and base: Two pieces, each 1¾ x 4⅛ in. (45 x 105mm)
Back: one piece, 3½ x 4⅛ in. (88 x 105mm)
From 3/16 in. (5mm) thick wood, cut two door pieces, each 2 1/16 x 3½ in. (52 x 88mm). Sand the edges of each cut piece.

2 Assemble the cabinet box as shown in the diagram, and glue the pieces together. Copy the templates for the legs and decorative boards onto paper, cut them out and draw round them on ⅛ in. (3mm) thick wood.

decorative board—front

decorative board—side

leg

3 Cut four legs, one front, and two sides, sand them and then glue them to the cabinet base. Once the glue is dry, sand the outside of the box, then color it with dark red acrylic paint. When dry, cover with black acrylic paint.

4 When dry, use fine-grit paper to rub the cabinet lightly, revealing glimpses of the red.

5 Attach the doors to the front of the box with masking tape. Attach hinges to the side pieces with small pins or tacks. Bend the hinges over the edge of the door and secure with pins.

6 Attach a decorative metal fretwork piece as a door lock. Use a fine brush and gold metallic paint to paint designs on the cabinet surface. Finish with acrylic varnish.

WALL PANEL AND COVING

1 For the wall panel, photocopy the fretwork layout guide onto paper and tape it to a sheet of glass. You will need to enlarge the design to fit the size of your wall—an enlargement of around 130 percent to 150 percent will probably be suitable. Tape stiff cream paper over the top, and shine a light up through the design.

2 With a sepia (brown) colored pen, trace the fretwork panel design onto the cream paper. Add hanging threads and tassels with a red colored pencil, using the picture as a guide. Cut out the panel and glue it to a ready-papered wall. Spray glue will give the smoothest finish, sprayed onto the back of the panel.

3 From white watercolor paper, cut a rectangle 1⅜ x 5⅛ in. (35 x 130mm). Using the photographs and Chinese or Japanese paintings as a guide, paint a simple scene with watercolor paints. Alternatively, cut a scenic panel from a greetings card. As a frame, add strips of patterned paper. Glue the panel to the wall inside the fretwork frame.

4 Copy the coving designs onto strips of cream paper using the technique described in steps 1 and 2. Repeat the design to give long strips. Cut them out using a craft knife. Glue the thick strip (lower coving) to the top of the wall. Glue the thin strip (upper coving) to the edge of a length of ⅛ in. (3mm) thick, ¼ in. (6mm) wide wood, cut to fit the top of your wall. Glue the wood to the ceiling.

upper coving layout guide

DRAPES

An impression of refinement is emphasized in the décor of this sitting room by the painted drapes in a trompe l'oeil style popular in the eighteenth century. Trompe l'oeil means fooling the eye into believing that a flat image is real or three-dimensional. In keeping with this style, these drapes are painted to give the impression of luxurious folded velvet framed by a golden fringe and tassels.

1 Cut a rectangular piece of thick blue cardboard to fit exactly within your window alcove. Glue small strips of wood to the walls and ceiling to hold the cardboard drapes when complete.

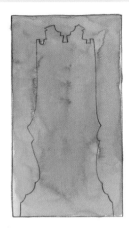

2 With a pencil, lightly sketch out the curtain shape, using this diagram as a guide.

3 Use dilute golden yellow acrylic paint to block out the bold areas of the gold fringe and tassels, and the fine curls on the valance. Use the picture as a guide.

4 Mix a little white paint into the golden yellow and use this to paint pale highlights where the yellow curtain edge is bunched up near the tiebacks and on the tassels. Add a little burnt umber-colored paint to a new dilute mix of golden yellow paint and mark in the shadows of the folds. Also use this color to mark in the details of the tassels and to define the edges of the fringe.

5 Mix a little white into some dilute mid-blue acrylic paint and use this to paint long pale highlights of the folds of the curtain fabric. Add a little dark blue paint to a new dilute mix of mid-blue paint and mark in the shadows of the folds. Pay particular attention to the areas just below the valance and above and below the tiebacks.

6 As a finishing touch, add a line of spots of red and blue paint along the edges of the drapes and around the tops of the tassels, to denote colorful braid. When the paint is dry, use a craft knife to cut out the shaped panel from the center of the drapes piece. Glue the drapes in place against the wooden strips on the walls and ceiling.

lower coving layout guide

Shaker work room

An oval box is an essential feature of a Shaker room.

The Shakers were a religious sect that originally derived from a small group of radical English Quakers. The group traveled from England to America in 1774 to escape persecution for their noisy ritual practices that included shaking, shouting, and dancing. As their numbers grew they settled in hard-working communities, from Maine to Indiana, and it was here that they were given the name "Shakers." Their motto, "Put your hands to work and hearts to God," expresses the essence of Shaker thinking. They chose to live separately from the "world's people" and to produce everything they needed for their own lives. They prized an uncomplicated lifestyle, and their interiors and handiwork have come to epitomize beauty through simplicity. They became known for their fine crafts and furniture making—everything motivated by respect for nature's resources unadorned by unnecessary decoration. Shaker interiors are characterized by airy rooms that are sparsely furnished with wooden items of fine quality. In the following chapter you will learn how to choose the tools, materials, and objects to create a Shaker room for your dollhouse.

THE BASICS

◄ MAKING A FLOOR
Fine-grain maple is ideal for an authentic Shaker floor. Oak is also suitable, if you can find pieces with an even color and without knots or over-large grain marks. Spruce or fine-grain pine can also be used. Because the choice of floor will have a marked effect on the overall color balance of the room, make sure you test your finish (oil or matte varnish) on a spare piece of your selected wood.

◄ THE WALLS
Plain, whitewashed walls give a fine, simple background against which your furniture and accessories can be displayed. Choose paint with a matte finish applied thinly and evenly, in plain white or with a touch of cream. Alternatively, walls can be clad in wood—narrow boards butted up to one another to cover the whole area. The wood can be left plain, or can be oiled, or sealed with a matte varnish.

► WAINSCOT
After installing the floor, a simple line of wainscot can be added around the base of the walls. This gives a feeling of solidity and serves to neaten the floor edges. Ready-molded wainscot lengths are available from many dollhouse suppliers in a range of colors and tones.

FURNITURE AND FITTINGS

▶ HANGING SHELF

An example of the Shaker belief that "Beauty rests on Utility," the clean lines of this shelf descend neatly from the peg rail surrounding the room. Instructions are on page 60.

▶ THE CLOCK

A clock, almost austere in its simplicity, hangs neatly on the peg rail. You can create a clock like this by following the instructions on page 59. Or add a hanging loop to the back of an existing clock to make your scene complete.

▶ SPECIAL FEATURES

In a plain room, the quality of the central features is vital. This iron stove was purchased from a specialist Shaker dollhouse supplier. It is typically rectangular and low, so that heavy logs can be easily placed inside. This model stands on a "stone" slab fashioned from air-drying modeling clay. The clay has been mottled with acrylic paints to give it a stone finish.

◀ WORK TABLE

A stable and practical little work table combines function with beauty. It is light enough to be moved easily around the room, yet carries two roomy drawers in which items such as mending or the half-finished household accounts could be stored away safely. Follow the instructions on page 61, to add drawers to a Shaker table of your own.

▼ SHAKER CHAIR

In Shaker design, functionality is everything. These chairs are built robustly in beautiful fine-grained maple wood. They illustrate the Shaker preoccupation with using wood efficiently, out of respect for nature's resources. These two chairs are built from the same basic design, one having added rockers to make a Shaker woman more comfortable whilst working on her crafts. Instructions for adapting a ladderback chair to a Shaker chair are on page 58.

◀ OVAL BOXES

No Shaker room would be complete without an oval box. Miniature versions can be made with strips of thin wood veneer, and used to store fruit, vegetables, or kindling for the fire. A small oval or round box would make the perfect container for needlework. You can learn how to make a Shaker box on page 61.

▶ CUPBOARDS AND CABINETS

Choose furniture in plain woods without paint or ornament. Shelves, simple cupboard doors, and wooden handles are all features to emphasize. If your room has an alcove, consider making a built-in cabinet. The efficient use of space was a standard feature of most Shaker rooms.

▶ SOFT FURNISHINGS

A plain-colored, hardwearing fabric has been chosen for a rug. Textural fabrics made from natural fibers—such as burlap, calico, or fine-weave tapestry canvas—are good choices. Synthetic fabrics can also be used as long as the colors do not look artificial. Some Shaker rugs included geometric and flower designs worked in two or three colors. Take a look in Shaker art books for examples.

ADD TO THE LOOK

▲ CLASSIC PEGRAIL

Rows of pegs lining the walls are a classic element of Shaker interior design. Used for hanging items—such as chairs, clocks, and shelves, in addition to coats and hats—pegs served to keep a variety of objects neatly out of the way. Choose a color of wood or wood stain that will contrast with the walls. Instructions are on page 59.

"Provide places for all your things, so that you may know where to find them day or night." The Shakers were almost obsessively tidy, and their homes held a multitude of chests, boxes, baskets, and other forms of storage. Turned wooden bowls and plates would hold fruit, vegetables, and other food.

A hanging Shaker candle can be made from a cake candle stuck into a metal ring and then glued to a wooden button. Drill holes in a hanging stick, glue the end to the button, and hang the candle on the peg rail.

THE SHAKER CHAIR

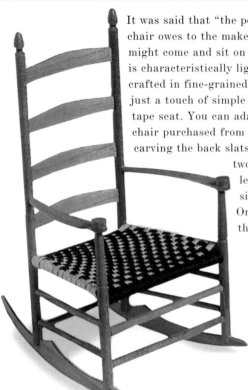

It was said that "the peculiar grace of a Shaker chair owes to the maker's belief that an angel might come and sit on it." The chair shown here is characteristically lightweight and graceful, crafted in fine-grained wood and finished with just a touch of simple decoration in its woven tape seat. You can adapt a plain ladderback chair purchased from a dollhouse store by carving the back slats to a gentle curve. Add two cross braces between the legs at the front and on the sides, and one at the back. Once you have finished, sand the model and varnish it.

ACORN FINIALS
The slender finials on the back posts and the mushroom turnings on the armrests are the signatures of traditional woodworking practice that Shaker craftsmen left in all their pieces. Follow the instructions to carve the finials; the mushroom turnings are made in a similar fashion.

ADDING ROCKERS
Trace the template below (enlarge or reduce to scale if necessary) onto thin paper. The arrows indicate where the chair legs should be attached. Cut out the template and draw round it twice on a sheet of 1⁄16 in. (2mm) thick wood. Cut out the shapes using a coping saw or sharp craft knife and sand smooth. Using a sharp knife, cut locating slots in the bottom of the chair legs, making sure that the cuts are of equal depth, no wider than the sanded rockers, and precisely in line from front leg to back. Glue the rockers in position, attaching both at the same time. Before the glue is quite dry, make sure the rockers are positioned symmetrically, and that the chair will stand up on the rockers without tipping. Adjust the position if necessary and leave the chair upside down to dry.

rocker template

❶ Use a sharp craft knife to scribe a line around the top of each post about ⅜ in. (10mm) in from the end.

❷ Carve away a little wood down to the scribed line, to shape the characteristic acorn finial. Sand smooth with fine-grit paper.

WOVEN SEAT
Although some Shaker chairs used sea grass (rush) seating, tape was the most common seating material. You can make an excellent likeness of a woven seat by following these steps, using a large needle and linen or embroidery floss in two contrasting colors, one light and one dark. Note that the diagrams refer to a frame seat (one that has a hole through the middle). If your chair has a blocked-in seat, the return thread for each woven line must be run along the undersurface of the chair. It is not difficult, just a little more work.

❶ Glue the end of the light-colored thread to the base of the chair, just under the seat. When dry, wind the thread neatly around the chair, the lines of thread running in the same direction and parallel to each other. When you reach the other end, glue the end of the thread out of sight under the chair and trim off any excess.

❷ Glue the end of the darker-colored thread to the chair just under the seat. Thread your needle and begin to weave. Go over three pale threads, then under three, and continue in this pattern to the end. Go once around the cross brace and come back to the start, weaving the same pattern along the way.

❸ Make three lines in this way. For the next three lines, start by going under three threads, then over, making a contrasting pattern to the first set of threads. Repeat this process until the chair seat is complete. Glue the end of the thread out of sight under the chair and trim off any excess.

HANGING CLOCK

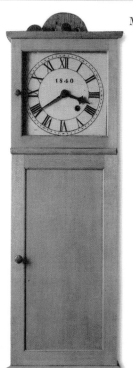

Most of the clocks for Shaker communities were manufactured by Benjamin or Isaac Young of Watervliet, NY. They were made with a pine case and hand-worked movement, both of which would display the classic Shaker traits of pride in workmanship and excellence in execution. Most of these clocks are still keeping time today, more than 160 years after they were built.

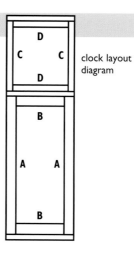

clock layout diagram

clock back template

clock face template

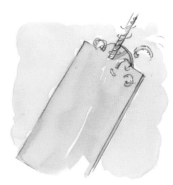

❶ From ⅛in. (3mm) thick wood, cut the following:
A: 2 pieces, each ⅛ x 1⁷⁄₁₆ in. (3 x 37mm)
B: 2 pieces, each ⅛ x ½ in. (3 x 13mm)
C: 2 pieces, each ¹⁄₁₆ x ¾ in. (2 x 19mm)
D: 2 pieces, each ¹⁄₁₆ x ⁹⁄₁₆ in. (2 x 15mm)
Main board: 1 piece, ¾ x 2⅜ in. (19 x 60mm)

❷ Sand smooth the cut edges of the wood. Draw or photocopy the clock face onto good-quality white paper. Cut out the square and glue it to the top of the main board.

❸ Lay the main board on a flat surface. Glue the other frame pieces onto the board, using the layout diagram as a guide. Cut ¾ in. (19mm) lengths of narrow molding and glue them at the top and bottom of the clock. Add a ¾ in. (19mm) strip between the clock face and case. Glue on two wooden beads as handles.

❹ Trace the clock back template onto paper and cut it out. With a pencil, draw round the shape on ⅛ in. (3mm) thick wood. Drill a hole in the position marked with a ¹⁄₁₆ in. (2mm) drill bit. Cut out the shape using a coping saw or craft knife and sand smooth the edges. Glue this piece to the back of the clock.

CLASSIC PEG RAIL

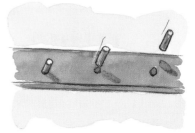

❶ Cut ¼ in. (6mm) wide strips of wood to run along the walls. Hold the strip up to the wall to judge exactly where you would like it to be. Make sure other items from the room are in place, so that the peg rail can run above the furniture.

❷ Use a ¹⁄₁₆ in. (2mm) drill bit to drill holes in the peg rail at regular intervals.

❸ On a protected surface roll a wooden barbecue skewer under the blade of a sharp knife. Press down as you roll to cut a ¼ in. (6mm) long peg from the skewer. Cut a number of pegs.

❹ Stain the rail and pegs, and glue the pegs into the rail holes. For shaped pegs, use a craft knife to shape the head of each peg, following instructions for acorn finials on the opposite page.

HANGING SHELVES

Traditionally, this style of Shaker shelf would be hung from a peg rail that would run around the walls of the room. Leather thongs would be threaded through holes in the sides of the shelf and then looped over the peg. These classic plain shelves would make a handsome addition to other work room or kitchen settings of the nineteenth and twentieth centuries. For other periods or styles, do not drill the hanging holes in step 1. Instead, attach the finished shelves directly to the wall with glue or brackets.

❶ Copy the side template onto paper, cut it out and draw round it twice on ⅛ in. (3mm) thick wood. Use a ⅛ in. (3mm) drill to make holes in the positions marked, then cut out the shapes marked by the solid line, with a fine coping saw.

❷ Using a sharp craft knife and a metal ruler, mark out the rectangles indicated by the dotted lines on the template. Run the knife along the sides of the rectangles repeatedly until you have cut into the wood to a little more than ½2 in. (1mm). These lines are stop cuts.

❸ With a small chisel, remove the wood inside the rectangles up to the stop cuts.

❹ For the shelves, cut the following:
Top shelf: ⁹⁄₁₆ x 2½ in. (15 x 65mm)
Middle shelf: ¾ x 2½ in. (19 x 65mm)
Bottom shelf: ⅞ x 2½ in. (22 x 65mm)
To create neat joints, on each shelf use a craft knife to mark a line a little more than ½2 in. (1mm) in from each end. Run the knife along the lines repeatedly until you have cut into the wood to a little more than ½2 in. (1mm). This line is a stop cut.

❺ With a small chisel, remove the ends of the wood up to the stop cut.

❻ Turn the shelves over and use a craft knife to mark a small rectangle ½2 x ¹⁄₁₆ in. (1 x 2mm) in each corner of the shelf. Cut until each rectangle is detached.

❼ Sand and stain all pieces, then assemble them as shown in the diagram. You may need to trim some of the joint pieces to create a good fit. Glue the pieces together and hang them from the peg rail with strips of thin leather or embroidery floss.

shelf side template

WORK TABLE

The Shaker belief that "beauty rests on utility" is exemplified by this attractive sewing table. A smooth maple-wood surface provides just enough space for one person's work and tools, and two smooth-running drawers ensure that additional fabrics, threads, pins, and scissors are always close at hand. At the end of the afternoon, the needlework can be packed neatly away. Choose a pedestal table with a graceful spindle and legs. With three legs, the table is guaranteed not to wobble, making it especially suitable as a stable counter.

ADDING HANGING DRAWERS

These drawers are designed for a table with a top approximately 2⅜ in. (60mm) square. For a larger table, make the drawers wider and longer. For a smaller table, make the drawers thinner and shorter.

1 For each drawer, from ⅛ in. (3mm) thick wood cut the following:
Front and back: ⁷⁄₁₆ × ⅝ in. (11 × 16mm)
Sides: ⁵⁄₁₆ × 1⅞ in. (8 × 48mm)
Base: ⅝ × 1⅞ in. (16 × 48mm)
With a ¹⁄₁₆ in. (2mm) drill bit, drill a hole in the center of the front piece.

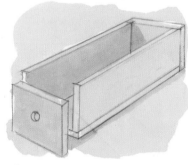

2 Varnish the pieces and then assemble and glue them as shown in the diagram.

3 Cut four runners from ¹⁄₁₆ in. (2mm) square wood, 2⅛ in. (54mm) long. Varnish and glue to each side of the drawers.

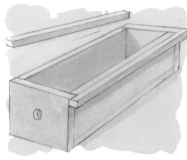

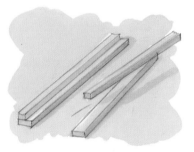

4 For each rail, cut an upright ¹⁄₁₆ × ⅛ × 2⅛ in. (2 × 3 × 54mm) and a horizontal ¹⁄₁₆ × ³⁄₃₂ × 2⅛ in. (2 × 4 × 54mm). Varnish, and glue them into an L-shape. Make four.

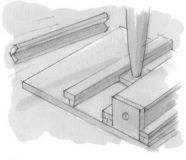

5 Place the table upside down and position the drawers upside down on top. Glue the rails over the top of the drawer runners. Leave to dry thoroughly. Insert a ready-made wooden handle in the front piece, or attach a small wooden bead.

A SHAKER BOX

For larger or smaller boxes, enlarge or reduce the template using a photocopier, then follow the instructions using a larger or smaller block in step 2. To make colored boxes, color the box components with watercolor paint well diluted with water before they are glued together. Leave to dry before gluing into shape.

1 Copy the templates onto paper and use a pencil to draw round them on thin wood veneer. Use a craft knife to cut out the pieces. Cut against a metal ruler to keep the long edges straight.

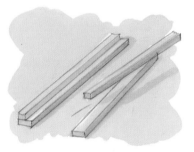

2 Wet the veneer then coil it around a circular or oval block, with the ends overlapping. Coil the rim piece on top, then the lid piece on top of that. Bind the veneer pieces with yarn to hold them in place. Leave to dry.

3 Remove the yarn and veneer from the block. Re-coil the box piece and glue into shape. Glue the rim piece around the top edge. Re-coil the lid piece and glue into shape.

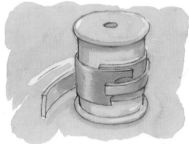

4 Using a pencil, draw round the lid and box pieces on thin wood veneer. Cut out the shapes using a craft knife, cutting inside the pencil line. Glue one piece on top of the lid and the other on the base of the box. Use fine-grit paper to smooth the edges.

5 For a finishing touch, use brass metallic paint to add tiny rivet marks, using the picture on page 56 as a guide.

box

rim

lid

Extend these pieces as far as you need to make a box of the desired size.
The lid and rim pieces should be slightly longer than the box pieces.

Small-town store

A small-town store was, and is, a very important part of community life in rural America. In the early twentieth century it was the place to which people from outlying villages and settlements would come to buy food and goods such as fabric, paint, pots and pans, and tools.

Other services were also available, such as the opportunity to make phone calls—something that we now take for granted in our own homes. But at a time when domestic phones were not yet common, a public phone available in a store was a crucial lifeline for many families.

The small-town store was also a place where people could pick up their post, news of local events, and, perhaps most importantly of all, gossip. Some families came only rarely to the town from their outlying farms, so it was a day out for the children and a special occasion for all. In the winter, the family might huddle around the stove while their large order was put together, enjoying a treat of candies or soda. In the summer, the children would sit on the steps outside waiting for their parents to finish the shopping. In this chapter, find out how to create the fixtures and fittings to put together a small-town store, and start to fill the shelves with a medley of goods, following the detailed instructions provided.

Pottery demi-johns to store home-made beer.

A collection of hessian sacks can be filled with dried seeds and beans.

THE BASICS

◀ MAKING A FLOOR
Worn floorboards indicate the passing of many feet over many years. Fit floorboards with visible nail holes, and finish by sanding thoroughly, staining, sanding again, and repeating until you have a suitably settled-in effect.

▼ TRAP DOOR
For the owners of the small-town store, having plenty of storage space was critical. The store is spacious, but irregular deliveries meant that the quantity of goods on site at any time was unpredictable. Outhouses were used for large items. A cellar was also available, especially for foods such as cheeses that needed to be kept cool, or goods such as valuable tools that needed to be kept clean and safe. This trapdoor leads to the storage area below.

◀ DRAWER UNIT
Practical shelves and drawers provide spaces for the goods to be displayed and stored neatly. Create broad shelving units from planks of ⅛ in (3mm) thick wood, and create a unit of drawers like these from the instructions on page 68.

FURNITURE AND FITTINGS

◀ DESK AND STOOL

The desk is a practical piece of furniture, mainly for use by the storekeeper. Because customers' incomes were minimal and sporadic, bills were often held on a tab. At the desk, a record of transactions was kept in a big ledger. Beside the desk a stool was provided for customers using the telephone. Instructions for the desk are on page 66 and for the stool on page 67.

▶ STOVE

Situated in the middle of the store and kept well away from flammable goods, this handsome stove provided warmth for the storekeeper and customers. Because shopping visits were infrequent, especially for members of outlying farming communities, shopping lists tended to be extensive. So the family would need to be in the store for a long time while their order was put together. Chairs were available for customers with the longest lists of all!

▼ CHAIR

These chairs are based on a simple fan-backed design, constructed from inexpensive wood and made entirely without ornament. They are plain and practical, suited to rough treatment and to all sizes and shapes of occupant.

▲ BOXES, PARCELS, SACKS, AND CRATES

Many food items suitable for long-term storage were available to buy in bulk at the small-town store. Potatoes, grains, seeds, and pulses could be bought economically in large sackfuls to last the winter. Other goods in this store are contained in boxes, brown-paper parcels, and crates. Instructions for these containers are on page 69.

◀ MAIL BOX

A postal service that reaches every household in the country is a luxurious development of the modern world. In the late nineteenth and early twentieth centuries, mail tended to be delivered to one central place—such as a town—to be collected by individuals when they visited there. Postal communications might come from the bank, the lawyer, agricultural companies, or family members in other states or countries. Create a copy of this mail box by following the instructions on page 67.

▲ PILES OF FABRICS

Women in farming communities often spent their evenings mending or making clothes. Scraps of leftover fabrics were used to create other items—such as patchwork quilts. In the small-town store, bolts of colorful fabrics were available—one of the rare occasions when money could be spent on something that was both practical and beautiful.

▶ FOOD

A mainstay of the store's income, food—such as apples and sausages—is great fun to create in miniature, using polymer clay. Twist strips of white and red clay together to make candy twists. Tins of food can be made from lengths of dowel painted silver and finished with paper labels. Fill shelves with tiny jars and bottles, and put cheese and bread on display in a glass cabinet.

▲ TOOL BARREL

For farmers and families who grew many of their own vegetables, tools were vital pieces of equipment and a common item in small-town stores. This barrel of large agricultural tools will make a useful addition to your store's supplies. The templates on the following pages will enable you to create shovels, spades, rakes, and hoes, easily made from wooden poles with shaped cardboard for the ends.

ADD TO THE LOOK

◀ LIGHTING

At the beginning of the twentieth century, electric lighting was available only to city dwellers and the very wealthy, so oil lamps were still the main source of light for many people. Because they got so hot, oil lamps had to have a protective backing. Paint two dollhouse plates with pewter metallic paint. Fix one to a small wooden wall bracket and one directly to the wall, and place the lamp on the horizontal plate. In this scene, black patches appear on the ceiling above the lamps, where carbon has made its mark.

Have fun collecting and making objects to fill your small-town store. All sorts of items are suitable—some necessities and some luxuries. This scene includes items as diverse as washboards, boxes of cigars, jars, and tins of food, a coffee grinder, bottles of candies, a workbox of tools, and tins of paint.

DESK

This desk is comfortable to work at, whether standing or sitting. Its sloped top has a ridge at the bottom to support a large leather-bound ledger, and the top ledge supports dip pens and a bottle of ink. Items such as extra paper, a money tin, spare ink, and pens can be neatly stacked inside the desk.

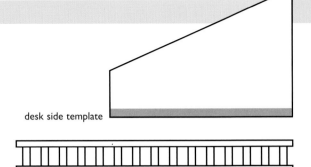

desk side template

desk grid gluing guide

❶ From ⅛ in. (3mm) thick wood, cut the following:
Lid: 1 piece, 3 in. (76mm) x 2⅝ in. (67mm)
Top strip: 1 piece, ⁵⁄₁₆ in. (8mm) x 3 in. (76mm)
Front: 1 piece, ½ in.(12mm) x 2½ in. (64mm)
Back: 1 piece, 1⅜ in. (35mm) x 2½ in. (64mm)
Foot rest: 1 piece, ⅞ in. (22 mm) x 2¾ in. (70mm)
Side struts: 2 pieces, each ¼ in. (6mm) x 2³⁄₁₆ in. (56mm)
Desk floor: 1 piece, 2³⁄₁₆ in.} (56mm) x 2¾ in. (70mm)
Sides: 2 pieces, using the desk side template
From ¼ in. (6mm) square wood, cut two front legs, each 2⅞ in. (73mm) long, and two back legs, each 3¾ in. (95mm) long. Lightly sand and stain all of the pieces.

❷ Glue strips of ¹⁄₁₆ in. (2mm) square wood along the bottom edge of the side, front and back pieces of the desk (marked in gray on the desk side template) as supports for the desk floor.

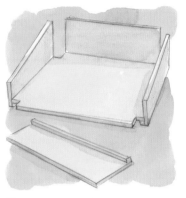

❸ Cut a ⅛ in. (3mm) square from each corner of the desk floor, and then glue it to the supports, making a box shape with empty corners.

❹ Trim the top of each front leg into an angle, so that they are 2¾ in. (70mm) tall at the front, and 2⅞ in. (73mm) at the back. In all four legs, cut a notch ¾ in. (19mm) up from the bottom, ⅛ in. (3mm) deep, ⅛ in. (3mm) wide, and ¼ in. (6mm) tall. Make sure that all of the slots will face in towards the center of the desk.

❺ Lay one front leg and one back leg on a flat surface. Glue a side strut in place with its ends in the slots. Compile the other legs and strut in the same way. Leave to dry thoroughly.

❻ Glue the legs to the desk and add the foot rest, glued with its ends resting on the side struts.

❼ Sand the bottom edge of the back of the desk lid to allow it to lie neatly at an angle to the top strip. Attach the desk lid to the top strip with two tiny hinges, and then glue the top strip to the top of the back legs, leaving a slight overhanging lip at the back of the desk.

❽ For the grid on the top of the desk, from ¹⁄₁₆ in. (2mm) square stained wood, cut two strips each 3 in. (76mm) long, and 15 strips each ³⁄₁₆ in. (5mm) long. Glue them together as shown in the desk-grid gluing guide, laying them on a flat surface. When dry, glue the whole unit to the top of the desk. Add another strip, 2¾ in. (70mm) long, along the bottom of the desk lid, and two drawer handles on the front of the desk. Varnish to finish.

STOOL

This attractive stool has a timeless design that is suitable for dollhouse scenes of many periods. Make a few stools to set around the store, with some placed by the counter where candy is served so that visiting children could perch upon them to enjoy a sugary treat.

stool top template

❶ From ³⁄₁₆ in. (5mm) thick wood, cut a 1³⁄₁₆ in. (30mm) diameter circle, using the template. Sand the edges smooth. From ⅛ in. (3mm) diameter dowel, cut four legs, each 1⅞ in. (48mm) long. Sand the bottom ends into slight tapers. From ¹⁄₁₆ in. (2mm) diameter dowel, cut two struts, each 3¹⁄₃₂ in. (24mm) long and two struts, each 1 in. (25mm) long Sand and stain all of the pieces.

❷ With a ¹⁄₁₆ in. (2mm) drill bit, make a hole halfway through each leg, ⅜ in. (10mm) up from the bottom. Glue a long strut between each pair of legs.

❸ Lie the legs flat and drill another hole halfway through each leg, ¾ in. (20mm) up from the bottom. Glue the two short struts to join the four legs together.

❹ Tape the top to a flat surface and drill holes halfway through it at the points marked on the template. Glue the legs in place, remove the tape, then varnish.

MAIL BOX

Created from notched shelves slotted together, this mail box is a classic addition to your store. Tiny letters can be made from scraps of colored paper stacked into the holes. Add stamps with a colored pen, and add a few black lines for an address.

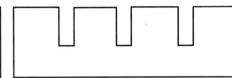

post box upright template   post box shelf template

❶ From cardboard, cut a rectangle 2 in. (50mm) x 2⅝ in. (67mm). From ⅛ in. (3mm) thick wood, cut the following:
Sides: 2 pieces, each 2 in. (50mm) x ¾ in. (19mm)
Top and bottom: 2 pieces, each 2¹³⁄₃₂ in. (61mm) x ¾ in. (19mm)
Lightly sand the wood and stain the cardboard and all of the pieces.

❷ Trace the upright and shelf templates onto paper and cut them out. Draw round them on ⅛ in. (3mm) thick wood and cut them out, using a craft knife to cut accurate slots. You will need three uprights and two shelves. Lightly sand and stain the pieces.

❸ Slot the uprights and shelves together and glue them as a unit to the cardboard, leaving a ⅛ in. (3mm) border around the edge.

❹ Glue the top, bottom, and side pieces to the shelves, and varnish to finish.

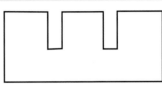

DRAWER UNIT

A sturdy set of drawers contains all the small things that are essential to self-sufficient living: nails, screws, hinges, spices, thread, buttons, tobacco, knife sharpeners, and tin openers. Drawerfuls of such oddments will be an intriguing addition to your store. If you do not feel confident to make a full set of drawers, you can give the impression of a drawer unit by gluing drawer fronts to a flat unit surface. Or make just one or two opening drawers amid fake drawers. The following instructions allow you to choose.

1 From ⅛ in. (3mm) thick wood, cut the following:
Back and front: 2 pieces, each 3⁷⁄₁₆ in. (88mm) × 7 in. (178mm)
Sides: 2 pieces, each 1⅜ in. (35mm) × 7 in. (178mm)
Top: 1 piece, 1⅝ in. (41mm) × 3½ in. (88mm)
Drawer fronts: 10 pieces, each ¾ in. (19mm) × 1¼ in. (32mm)
Internal supports: from ¼ in. (6mm) square wood, cut 4 pieces, each 7 in. (178mm)
Drawer handles: from ⅛ in. (3mm) square wood, cut 10 pieces, each ½ in. (12mm) long
Lightly sand and stain all of the pieces.

2 If you wish to make drawers that can open, use a pencil and ruler to draw ten drawer holes on the front piece, using the layout guide. Each hole should be 1⅛ in. (28mm) × ⁹⁄₁₆ in. (15mm). Use a sharp knife to cut out the holes.

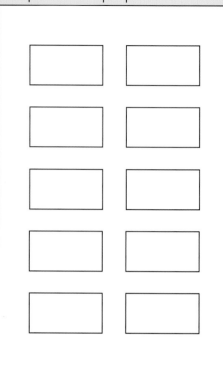

Right: Drawers layout guide, reproduced smaller than actual size.

3 Cut a rectangle, 2¾ in. (70mm) wide × 2 in. (50mm) tall out of the bottom edge of the front piece. Assemble and glue the main pieces of the drawer unit together as shown in the diagram, with internal supports to keep the corners square.

4 Glue strips of ⅛ in. (3mm) wide, ¹⁄₃₂ in. (1mm) thick wood strip (ready stained) to the edges of the unit using the photograph as a guide.

5 To make drawers that do not open, lay the drawer fronts in a regular arrangement on the drawer unit, then glue them in place. Glue a drawer handle to each drawer front. Varnish to finish.

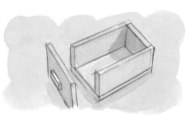

6 To make drawers that open, from ¹⁄₁₆ in. (2mm) thick wood, cut the following:
Backs: 10 pieces, each ½ in. (12mm) × ¹⁵⁄₁₆ in. (23mm)
Sides: 20 pieces, each ½ in. (12mm) × 1¼ in. (32mm)
Bases: 10 pieces, each 1 ¹⁄₁₆ in. (27mm) × 1¼ in. (32mm)
Assemble and glue the drawers together as shown in the diagram. Add handles as in step 5, and varnish to finish. Try the drawers in the holes and sand lightly to adjust the sizes to fit. You may need to add small block supports inside the face unit to support each drawer.

TOOLS IN BARREL

Barrels are an attractive storage feature of this small-town store. They can be stacked full of food such as apples, or filled with larger items like these agricultural tools. Create a barrel from slats of wood held together by glue and narrow barrel hoops. Some barrel hoops can be left plain. Alternatively, color the hoops with black or metallic paint.

BARREL

❶ From ³⁄₁₆ in. (5mm) thick wood, cut 15 strips (lathes), each ⁵⁄₁₆ in. (8mm) wide and 2³⁄₈ in. (60mm) long. Trim each lathe to be slightly thinner at both ends. Sand smooth and then color with a dark oak stain.

❷ For a 1¾ in. (45mm) diameter barrel, use a 1³⁄₈ in. (35mm) diameter mold (such as a round bottle, tin, or cardboard tube. Tape the lathes to the bottle, then run a little glue between each lathe. For a larger barrel, use more lathes; for a smaller one, use fewer (and shorter) lathes.

❸ Add strips of ¹⁄₃₂ in. (1mm) thin wood as hoops around the barrel. When thoroughly dry, remove the bottle and glue a 1³⁄₈ in. (35mm) diameter circle of wood inside the bottom of the barrel.

TOOLS

❶ From ¹⁄₈ in. (3mm) dowel, cut several tool handles, each 3 in. (75mm) long. Paint one end with silver metallic paint, to a length of about ⅝ in. (16mm).

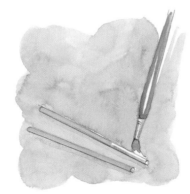

❷ Trace the tool templates onto paper and cut them out. Draw round them on cardboard and cut them out. Glue to the end of the tool handles and color with silver metallic paint.

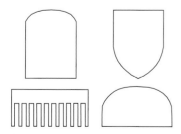

tools templates

STORAGE AND PACKAGING

Fill the tops of the shelving units with stacks of boxes and parcels, and stack the floor with crates and sacks. Remember that a successful storekeeper would miss no opportunity to stock items to satisfy his or her regular clients, and would waste no space if something could be put on display to tempt new customers.

BOXES

Trace or photocopy the box base and lid templates onto paper and cut them out. Draw round them on thin card stock, score along the dotted lines, and cut out the shape. Fold up the box and glue the tabs in place.

PARCELS

Cut sections of wood strip and wrap them neatly in brown paper. Glue the ends of the paper in place. Tie thin string around some of them, and add labels. Stack them on top of the shelving units.

SACKS

Cut two rectangles of coarse-weave fabric. Sew them together around three edges and turn right side out. Fill with dry seeds or beans and sew shut, tucking the raw edges of fabric inside as you go.

CRATES

From ¹⁄₁₆ in. (2mm) thick wood, cut 2 side pieces, each 1 in. (25mm) x 1¾ in. (45mm); and 2 end pieces, each 1 in. (25mm) square. Score with lines, and then glue the pieces together on top of a 1⅛ in. (29mm) x 1¾ in. (45mm) rectangle of cardboard. Add two ⅛ in. (3mm) wide strips of ¹⁄₁₆ in. (2mm) thick wood vertically on each side.

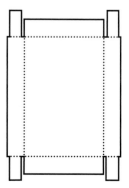

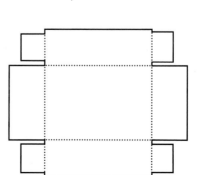

box base template   box lid template

American settler's parlor

A hand-embroidered rug with geometric designs brings a warm hue to the room.

Pretty printed fabrics can be used for curtains and upholstery.

The interior of a nineteenth-century settler's house is characterized by simplicity and practicality, with only a few quiet touches of comfort and decoration. Wastefulness had no place in a household that was built on hard work and commitment. Settlers were not wealthy—they sought a livelihood on the land and therefore had little spare capital to invest in grand features or fittings for their houses. Indeed, such extravagances were often frowned upon, with a hint of puritanical zeal. The community lived by the work of its hands, raised crops, livestock, and children, and knew how to make the very most of natural materials—such as wood, stone, and leather. They truly understood the qualities of these materials. A stone fireplace was not only attractive and solid, it would also hold the warmth over the long winters, when the fire was never allowed to go out. Wooden walls could be renewed and extended with planks readily available from the surrounding forests, and hardwearing leather could be used as the upholstery for a sturdy chair that would last for many, many years. In this chapter, you can learn how to capture the pioneer spirit of a settler's house, with the characteristic furniture and fittings that will bring the scene to life.

THE BASICS

◀ **MAKING A FLOOR**
Long planks of wood were very valuable, and so were used for important construction projects such as house walls, outhouses, and second-storey floorboards. For a ground-floor room, smaller tiles of wood were sufficient and gave a parquet-like finish—a warm lining for the floor. A single hardwearing woolen rug added a touch of color to the room.

▲ **THE WALLS**
Large planks butted up to one another form the interior cladding of the solid walls of this cabin-like house. The outer walls might also be formed from planks, but if the family had decided to settle on the land, then the exterior wooden walls would be replaced by stone.

▼ **BEAMS**
A crossbeam cut from an enormous oak or redwood tree forms the backbone of the room's construction. Resting on other large beams set into the walls, it acts as the support for rafters that hold the floorboards for the room upstairs. The ceiling is not finished with any further covering, avoiding waste of materials.

FURNITURE AND FITTINGS

◀ THE CHAIR

No single style of chair epitomizes the choice of a nineteenth-century settler. Collections of furniture were put together from what the family could make or afford at the time. Some items were treasured heirlooms and some were made by members of the community. This sturdy little chair was probably built by a member of the family from off-cuts of wood, and covered in home-produced leather. Instructions are on page 74.

▶ SIDEBOARD

In a small house, tidiness is essential, especially when a large family shared the space. The few items that the family possessed, such as china, linen, and glassware, were stored away carefully in a practical sideboard. There was little need or place for ornaments in such a household.

◀ DOOR

A practical door can be put together from wooden boards glued together and strengthened with crosspieces. Over the years, the boards might shrink and crack, so they would often be repaired, and cracks would be filled to keep out the drafts. Instructions for making a wooden door are on page 77.

▶ DROP-LEAF TABLE

A practical drop-leaf table served as a place for the family to eat together, but also as a surface upon which schoolwork or needlework could be laid out. In this scene on pages 78 to 79, a tea set has been prepared for a rare moment of relaxation—probably on a Sunday when the whole family took a day of rest.

▶ WINDOW

Although windows had to be large enough to let in natural light, they could not be excessively large because of the bitter winter that beset the family every year. It might snow so much that the windows were completely covered, and so they had to be small and strong enough to withstand this pressure. Pretty curtains might be replaced in winter with a thicker, heavier set to keep the warmth in. Instructions for this window are on page 75.

▲ TEA SET AND KETTLE

An attractive tea set was one of the few luxuries that this family possessed. Water was heated in a kettle on the fire and kept warm on an iron stand on the hearth.

▼ BIBLE BOX

A Bible box was a common feature in a settler's parlor. Work was the motivating force in the household, but rest was also valued, and Sunday was a special day for the family to spend time together. Children might be allowed to play with a homemade Noah's Ark toy, and a Bible would be lifted reverentially from its box, so that stories and lessons from its pages could be shared by the family.

▼ PICTURE

Pioneer families were proud of their family history. The few luxuries that they allowed themselves might include one or two paintings to remind them of their ancestors.

ADD TO THE LOOK

▶ FIREPLACE

A stone chimneybreast forms the focal point of the room. During long, cold winter nights the fire was the only source of warmth, so the fireplace is very open and broad, allowing the family to gather around. Water would be heated over the flames for cooking and washing.

The presence of so many different types of candle holder around the room indicates that in the evening the family continued with activities such as darning, reading, and carpentry. A chandelier, floor-standing candelabra, and hand-held candleholders are all suitable items for a room of this period. Instructions for making a chandelier and hand-held candlestick are on page 77.

CHAIR

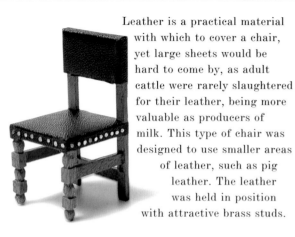

Leather is a practical material with which to cover a chair, yet large sheets would be hard to come by, as adult cattle were rarely slaughtered for their leather, being more valuable as producers of milk. This type of chair was designed to use smaller areas of leather, such as pig leather. The leather was held in position with attractive brass studs.

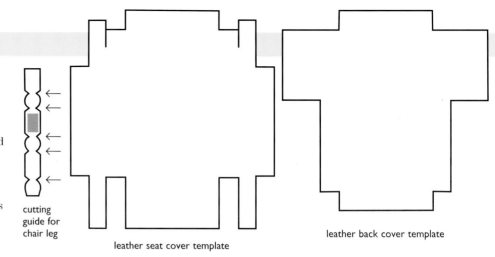

cutting guide for chair leg

leather seat cover template

leather back cover template

❶ From ³⁄₁₆ in. (5mm) thick wood, cut the following:
Back legs: 2 pieces, each ⅛ in. (3mm) × 2¾ in. (70mm)
Front legs: 2 pieces, each ³⁄₁₆ in. (5mm) × 1⁵⁄₁₆ in. (34mm)
Back rest: 1 piece, ¾ in. (20mm) × 1⅜ in. (36mm)
Back strut: 1 piece, ⅛ in (3mm) × 1¹⁄₁₆ in (26mm)
Side strut: 2 pieces, ⅛ in. (3mm) × 1⁵⁄₁₆ in (34mm)
From ³⁄₁₆ in. (5mm) thick wood, cut a 1⅜ in. (36mm) square for the seat. From each front corner, remove a ³⁄₁₆ in. (5mm) square. From each back corner, remove a rectangle ⅛ in. (3mm) × ³⁄₁₆ in. (5mm), the long edges parallel to the back of the chair.
Cut a piece of ¹⁄₁₆ in. (2mm) thick foam the same shape and size.

❷ Use a knife to scribe five lines around each front leg at the positions marked on the cutting guide. Carve a little wood away from each side down into the scribed lines, shaping each leg as outlined in the guide. Sand smooth.

❸ Cut a slot in each front leg in the position marked in gray on the guide. Cut halfway through the leg. On each back leg, cut a similar slot, starting 1¹⁄₁₆ in. (17mm) up from the base.

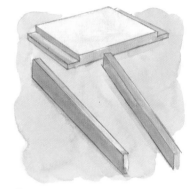

❹ Cut a ⅛ in. (3mm) deep, ³⁄₁₆ in. (5mm) wide notch into each side of the back rest.

❺ Assemble and glue the chair together as shown above. The back strut can be positioned and glued without slots. Varnish to finish. Glue the foam on top of the seat piece.

❻ Copy the seat-cover template onto paper, cut it out and draw round it on leather-effect fabric. Cut it out and fit it to the chair, with the long tabs to the back. Copy the back-cover template, cut out as before, and fit as shown.

❼ Glue the fabric to the chair. On the seat, fold the tabs around the front and back. When dry, use a needle to make holes for the brass pins. Insert short brass-headed pins using the photograph as a guide.

The back of the chair, showing the brass pins.

WINDOW

This attractive window is set into a thick stone wall, clad with wooden planks. When framed by colorful curtains, it is a bright spot in an otherwise somber room. Choose an attractive piece of wood for the windowsill and finish it with varnish to catch the light from outside for the best effect.

❶ From ³⁄₁₆ in. (5mm) wood, cut a length as a windowsill, to slot neatly into the window hole, overhanging at the front by ⅛ in. (3mm). Cut strips of ³⁄₁₆ in. (5mm) wood to line the sides and top of the window hole without an overhang. Trim a ⅛ in. (3mm) strip off the back edge of each one, and then glue them together in a frame.

❷ Cut a piece of ⅛ in. (3mm) thick glass or Perspex ¼ in. (3mm) smaller than the frame on each side. Cut ⅛ in. (3mm) square wood strips to fit around the glass, then glue them to the back of the frame.

❸ Draw a diamond pattern onto the glass or Perspex with permanent black felt-tip pen.

❹ Glue the frame into the window hole, position the plastic or glass, and hold them in place with an external frame you have made from strips of ³⁄₁₆ in. (5mm) thick wood.

❺ On the inside of the window, cut a length of wooden molding as an upright and glue it in place. Cut two more lengths as crosspieces and glue them in place. Varnish the wood.

CURTAINS

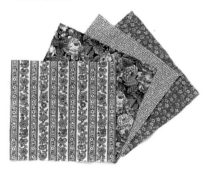

❶ Cut two rectangles of thin cotton fabric, each 1³⁄₁₆ in. (30mm) longer than the height of the window, and as wide as three-quarters the width of the window. Fold and sew a hem along each edge.

❷ Cut ten 1³⁄₁₆ in. (30mm) lengths of ³⁄₁₆ in. (5 mm) wide ribbon in a color to match the curtains. Fold each piece of ribbon in half. Sew five at regular intervals to the back of each curtain.

❸ Curtain pole: Use an awl to make a hole on either side of the window. Screw in two small brass screw eyes. From ⅛ in. (3mm) diameter dowel, cut a piece ¾ in. (20mm) wider than the space between the screw eyes. Use sandpaper to taper each end slightly. Varnish to finish.

❹ Insert the pole through one ribbon loop, then the first screw eye, then all of the rest of the curtain loops on one curtain. Then insert the pole through all but the last of the curtain loops of the second curtain. Slide the end of the pole through the other screw eye, then the final loop. Secure the single ribbon loops at each end with a little glue.

FIREPLACE STONES EFFECT

An impressive stone fireplace is the centerpiece of the room, around which chairs can be arranged for their occupants to make the most of the fire's light and warmth. The following instructions show you how to adapt an existing fireplace by the addition of a beam, and how to create a stone effect from air-drying clay. Alternatively, cover the fireplace with stone-effect paper available from dollhouse suppliers.

1 From ³⁄₁₆ in. (5mm) thick, 1 in. (25mm) wide wood, cut a beam as long as the width of the chimneybreast. Use a chisel or craft knife to shave pieces from the surface to give the impression of the beam having been shaped with a traditional tool such as an adze. Stain with dark oak color. Glue the beam to the chimneybreast, just above the fireplace.

2 Above and below the beam, press air-drying clay onto the surface of the wall, including the inside faces of the pillars on either side of the fireplace. Use the end of a piece of cardboard to mark out the lines of the stones. Make lines that run around the corners of the pillars on either side of the fire, to indicate large stones.

3 When the clay is dry, color the whole clay area with mid-gray acrylic paint. Add a little ochre paint to the gray mix and stipple the surface of the stones unevenly. Add a little dark blue into the mix and repeat until you achieve a pleasing effect.

NOTE

A hearthstone can be created from a section of slate tile set into the floor. Alternatively, press out more air-drying clay to form a hearth shape. When dry, color as for the fireplace stones above.

BIBLE BOX

For a small item such as a Bible box, it is worth investing in a beautiful piece of wood. This will enable you to create a polished surface, and it will be a joy to carve with a tiny chip-work design on the front panel. Choose a fine-grain wood, such as walnut or boxwood, which both respond well to fine carving.

1 From ⅛ in. (3mm) wood, cut the following:
Front and back: Two pieces, each ¾ in. (20mm) x 2 in. (50mm)
Sides: Two pieces, each ¾ in. (20mm) x 1 in. (25mm)
Lid and base: Two pieces, each 1 ⁵⁄₁₆ in. (34mm) x 2⅛ in. (54mm)

cross motif
pattern

2 Using the pattern as a guide, use a craft knife to mark out the cross shape on the front piece, letting the blade go in to a depth of about ½ in. (1mm).

3 Use a chisel to chip away wood between the scribed lines of the central design. Use the craft knife to trim away more wood around the outer line in a narrow groove.

4 Assemble and glue the box together as shown. Varnish to finish. Countersink two hinges into the back edge of the box and lid, and attach with tiny pin nails.

DOOR

A strong wooden door was an essential feature of an American settler's house, to keep in the warmth and act as security. Planks of wood can be butted together to form a sturdy structure, braced by two cross pieces and an additional vertical plank. Tiny brass and white-metal hooks, available from specialist dollhouse suppliers, can be fitted to the upper cross piece and are ideal for hanging tiny coats and hats.

1 Measure the height of your doorway and cut several narrow planks of 3/16 in. (5mm) thick wood to this length— enough to fill the width of the door. Shave some slivers of wood from the edges of the planks to give them a hand-finished look.

2 Stain the planks then lay them on a flat surface and glue them together. Wedge them between heavy books to keep the joints tight while drying.

3 From 1/8 in. (3mm) thick wood, cut two strips 3/4 in. (20mm) wide to run across the door, and one to run upright between them. Stain, then glue in place. Fit a dollhouse handle following the manufacturer's instructions.

4 Cut two shallow rectangular notches in the doorframe to hold the hinges, and two in the door. Fit the hinge with small flat-headed pin tacks.

CHANDELIER AND CANDLESTICK

The following designs are suitable to hold tiny birthday-cake candles. Alternatively, cut short sections of 1/8 in. (3mm) diameter dowel and paint them white. Give the impression of wicks with flecks of black paint on top. For a truly authentic finish, make your own candles by dipping black thread repeatedly into molten wax and shaping the resulting candle with your fingers.

CHANDELIER

1 For each of six candles, glue a short length of 3/16 in. (5mm) diameter plastic tube to a 1/2 in. (12mm) dollhouse saucer. Prepare a central wooden bead or small acorn light-pull by hanging it from a length of necklace chain.

2 Cut six 1 1/8 in. (28mm) lengths of 3/16 in. (5mm) wide metal strip. Bend each strip into a shallow S-shape. With quick-drying contact adhesive, glue the ends to the wooden bead. Glue the saucers to the ends and color with black metallic paint.

HAND-HELD CANDLESTICK

1 Glue a short length of 3/16 in. (5mm) diameter plastic tube to a 5/8 in. (16mm) diameter dollhouse bowl. Cut a narrow strip of cardboard, curl it and glue it to the bowl, as a handle. Paint the whole piece with black metallic paint.

NOTE

Brass candlesticks are also suitable for this nineteenth-century scene. These can be bought from specialist dollhouse suppliers. Or you could color a wooden or plastic candlestick with brass metallic paint.

Fine porcelain for
a special meal.

A classic Victorian
grandfather clock.

Victorian
dining room

Nineteenth-century Victorian England saw the rapid expansion of towns and cities, with housing developments springing up to cater for people moving into the cities to seek work in factories. The houses, like the objects produced in the factories, were mass-produced. Many houses were built in terraces—rows of houses joined together with shared walls and identical fittings, such as windows and doors. Many of these houses were built for people working in the factories. There were also larger and grander houses, such as this one, that included servants' quarters.

This household is occupied by a family that might have owned a factory. They are comfortably wealthy and are likely to have employed servants to take over the household tasks. Their house benefits from the conveniences that accompanied town living, such as gas lighting and running water. Decorative features also reflect the spirit of the time—manufactured repeat-pattern wallpaper, furniture made from tropical hardwoods, and an oriental rug shipped in from across the globe—demonstrating the rise of international trade. This chapter shows you how to create or adapt objects suitable to this Victorian scene.

THE BASICS

◀ MAKING A FLOOR
A polished floor in a parquet design is particularly appropriate for a Victorian house, giving a beautiful shiny surface on which to place a rug and fine mahogany furniture. Many designs of floor paper, such as the one pictured left, are available from many dollhouse suppliers. this one is a traditional herringbone design—a tesselating zigzag pattern created with two colors of wooden tiles. A square wood-tile pattern would also be appropriate.

◀ THE WALLS
In the nineteenth century, new methods of printing and mass production meant that even people who were not particularly wealthy could afford attractive wallpapers—usually floral designs with a strong repeat pattern or designs incorporating foliage and birds. These samples are wallpapers widely available from dollhouse suppliers. Chair and picture rails can be made from wooden molding strips. For more details of how to decorate the walls of a Victorian room, see page 85.

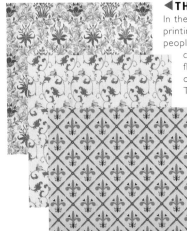

CEILING
Decorative plasterwork is also a classic feature of Victorian town houses. Advances in manufacturing techniques meant that ceiling roses, patterned coving, and cornice pieces became widely available. At dollhouse scale, patterned plasterwork can be imitated using textured wallpaper designed for a full-size house. The paper in this room has an attractive raised geometric pattern perfectly suited to a large area such as the upper walls and ceiling.

FURNITURE AND FITTINGS

▶CHAIR

Furniture in a middle-class Victorian household was good quality, but not extravagant; only the very wealthy could afford to commission hand-made furniture. Manufacturing techniques developed quickly in the nineteenth century, with furniture beginning to be mass-produced and made from hardwoods imported from across the world. Mahogany was a much sought-after wood with a rich red-brown color.

▲THE FOOD

The dinner served at this Victorian meal is traditional roast beef served on a large oval plate. The crockery is a traditional blue and white Chinese pattern, probably for everyday use. A set of more expensive china would be stored away for special occasions. Other suitable tableware for this meal includes lacey placemats cut from a larger piece of machine lace, china tureens, and a gravy boat.

▶MIRRORS AND PICTURES

Beautiful picture frames, with ornate detail, are available from most dollhouse suppliers. A large gilt-framed mirror fits perfectly above the fireplace. Portraits of people and animals can be framed with scraps of wooden molding, which have been cut into miters at the corners for a neat fit. This is best achieved by using a small miter block. Before gluing them together, paint the pieces with gold metallic enamel paint to mimic gilding.

▲TABLE

A Victorian dining set of table and chairs was a popular wedding present to establish a young couple in their new home. Created from the same wood as the chairs, a large mahogany table had an attractive polished surface that was protected from spills by a satin runner (as above) or a linen tablecloth. Instructions for creating a tablecloth are on page 82.

LIGHTING

Commercially produced gas lamps and flame-effect candles are suitable for a Victorian house, although a house set in the last few decades of the nineteenth century might also have electric lighting. A hand-held gas lamp is a nice touch for the lady of the house to carry with her in the dark hallway.

◀DRINKS TABLE

A plentiful supply of wine was a must for the Victorian host. This drinks table carries space for wine bottles and a hanging mechanism for up to sixteen tiny stemmed wine glasses. Instructions for making this table are on page 85.

◀GONG

The servants of the house were responsible for preparing the dining table and food ready for meals. When the room was ready, the gong was sounded to summon the family to eat, leaving the servants to withdraw to their own simple meal set out in the kitchen. Instructions for the gong are on page 84.

◀RUG

During the nineteenth century, trade with countries around the world flourished, including many craft items from Turkey and China, known for their beautiful and colorful rugs. The rug in the picture is Chinese, incorporating woven silks that create a classic pattern. This effect can be achieved by sewing together a patchwork-style rug from woven satin ribbons and embroidered brocade. Instructions are on page 83.

ADD TO THE LOOK

◀FIREPLACE

If your room has no chimneybreast, consider adding one by inserting a large block of wood against one wall (usually a side wall). Once glued in place, it can be made to blend in with the room by covering it in wallpaper and disguising the top and bottom joins with strips of coving and wainscot. Commercially produced fireplaces usually come complete with the plasterwork surround, the fireplace backing, and usually a built-in hearth. Add the fireplace when the chimneybreast is in place.

It was the job of the housemaid, at the bottom of the household's pecking order, to get up before everyone else each morning and make up the fires ready for the day. Brass fire irons and a coalscuttle, available from dollhouse suppliers, will complete the fireside scene.

DINING TABLECLOTH

A mahogany dining table was the centerpiece of a Victorian dining room. In the evening, servants would set the table for a formal meal. This project shows how to create a tablecloth with drapes and folds—the perfect backdrop for a Victorian dinner party.

MAKING THE FOOD

• Food can be created from polymer clay. Prepare the clay models on cardboard, then bake to harden following manufacturer's instructions. You can bake them on the cardboard, which will survive the low heat.

• To create gravy, use liquid plastic (available from dollhouse suppliers), which sets solid after about an hour. This can also be used to make a soup.

1 Place the table upside down on a piece of thin white cotton cloth. Use a hard pencil to draw around the table, leaving a 2 in. (50mm) border. Cut out the shape.

2 Mix wood glue with water— approximately half and half. Wash your hands and then dip the cloth into the glue mixture. When it is soaked, lift it out and remove the excess glue by running the cloth through your fingers until no drips remain.

3 Drape the cloth over the table. Encourage it to fall into natural folds, and carefully smooth out any wrinkles in the top surface. Leave to dry thoroughly. If any drips form, they can be removed with a knife or scissors once dry.

UPHOLSTERED CHAIR

The upholstery of a Victorian chair is an opportunity to introduce interesting textiles into the room. This chair has been upholstered with ivory satin cut from a length of ribbon. Colorful ribbon could also be chosen to match the patchwork ribbon rug (see page 83). Other suitable materials include fine plush velvet and cotton with a brushed surface. Woven braids also offer beautiful patterns that look very attractive on a chair seat; although thickly embroidered braids will prove too bulky to use.

1 Remove the seating board from the chair and cut away any covering and padding.

RUG

This richly colored rug shows the Victorian love of opulent textiles. Created from pieces of satin ribbons, embroidered brocade, and ready-made fringe, it is easy to create and is an impressive furnishing to brighten up a dining room. Pieces of the same ribbon can also be used to give the room a unified color scheme: the dusky pink ribbon could be used to cover the seats of the chairs, whereas the dark red braid could be used as an edging for cushions.

1 Cut the following:
Center: from 1½ in (38mm) wide patterned ribbon, cut two pieces, each 5 in. (127mm)
Sides: from 1¼ in. (32mm) wide dusty pink ribbon cut two pieces, each 5 in. (127mm)
Ends: from 1¼ in. (32mm) wide dusty pink ribbon cut two pieces, each 6 in. (152mm)
Fringe: from ready-made cotton or silk fringing, cut two pieces, each 5½ in. (140mm)

ADDING A FRINGE

- In Victorian times, fringes were a popular addition to textile items such as rugs and drapes, giving a rich and luxurious finish.

- Ready-made fringing is available from needlework stores. It is sold as trimming and usually comes with one woven edge that can be hidden behind the fabric. Use tiny stitches to attach the fringe to the fabric hem, or run a line of stitches along the edge, going all the way through.

2 With tiny stitches and pink thread (catching just a few threads at a time), sew the two central ribbons and the two side ribbons together into one panel, keeping the work as flat as possible.

3 Use a warm iron to press flat. Lay an end piece in position on top of the rug and pin it. Turn under the raw ends and use a line of tiny running stitch to attach it, using dusty pink thread. Press again.

4 Using running stitch and dark thread sew a line of textured braid along the center of each side panel and on to the end panels, making extra stitches at the ends to prevent the braid from fraying.

5 Using running stitch and dusty pink thread, sew a line of fringe to each end of the rug.

2 Cut a square of foam the same size as the seating board and glue it in place. On the underside of the board, make a frame of double-sided sticky tape.

3 Cut a square of fabric or ribbon 1 in. (25mm) larger than the seating board. Fold it around the board, securing the edges to the sticky tape.

4 Trim off excess fabric and glue loose edges in place with white glue. Fit the seat back into the chair, using a skewer to push awkward folds of fabric into place.

A MAHOGANY CHAIR

- The rich red-brown of mahogany wood is a classic feature of a Victorian dining room. If your chairs are a paler color, sand them to remove any varnish. Use a knife to scrape away varnish or glue in awkward corners and joints.

- Stain the chair with mahogany wood dye, or paint with dark red-brown acrylic paint. Allow to dry.

- Seal with acrylic varnish. Take care not to start any upholstery work before the paint, stain, and varnish are thoroughly dry.

GONG

A metallic gong is a beautiful addition to a Victorian dining room. Created from strips of shaped wood, with carved uprights cut from dollhouse banisters, hang a large button or circle of wood from the frame to complete the effect.

❶ Copy the foot template on to paper, cut it out and draw round it four times on ⅛ in. (3mm) thick wood. Use a craft knife to cut out the feet.

gong foot template

❹ The gong can be made from a large smooth-faced wooden button (with the shank trimmed off) or from a 1⅛ in. (29mm) diameter circle of ³⁄₁₆ in. (5mm) thick wood. A texture can be added by placing the head of a nail on the gong surface and hitting the pointed end with a hammer. Repeat across the face of the wood. Paint the button or wood with brass metallic enamel paint. With a needle, make two holes in the top bar of the hanging frame and insert two tiny brass pins (sold as dollhouse hinge nails). Glue a hanging thread to the gong.

❷ For the uprights, cut two lengths from ready-made dollhouse banisters, each approximately 1⅞ in. (48mm). Choosing matching sections that have a knob at each end, cut a shallow slot into each upright just below the top knob, and then another above the bottom knob, ⅛ x ³⁄₁₆ in. (3 x 5mm).

❸ From ⅛ in. (3mm) thick wood, cut two rectangles, each ³⁄₁₆ x 1¼ in. (5 x 32mm). Stain the wooden pieces. When dry, assemble and glue the frame as shown in the diagram. Where the feet will meet the uprights, use sandpaper to flatten the upright surfaces before gluing.

❺ With a needle, make a hole in the side of the frame and screw in a tiny hook, available from specialist dollhouse suppliers. Make a beater from a small stick, with a scrap of white felt wound and glued around the end. Cut a shallow groove around the end and attach a hanging thread.

❻ As a finishing touch, use brass metallic enamel paint to color details of the frame: see picture as a guide.

WALLS

The walls in this room are divided by the dark lines of a picture (upper) rail and the chair (lower) rail created with strips of mahogany colored molding. Below the chair rail is a striped wrapping paper; above the chair rail is commercially produced dollhouse wallpaper; above the picture rail is textured wallpaper designed for a full-size house, perfect in this situation to imitate decorative plasterwork. Around the top of the walls add plasterwork coving (pictured left), available from specialist dollhouse suppliers.

❶ To gauge what height to set the chair and picture rails, cut strips of molding ready for the rails. Stick them to the walls temporarily with reusable adhesive, and adjust them until they are in a satisfying position. Draw lines on the wall along the top edge of each rail to record the positions.

DRINKS TABLE

Social occasions were an important feature of life for a wealthy Victorian household. Visiting family members or business colleagues would be invited to share in an evening of fine food and conversation, fueled by a plentiful supply of wine. This drinks table is a perfect item for such an occasion. Guests would be able to help themselves to a glass and refill at their leisure from the bottles on top.

1 Copy template A on to paper and cut it out. Draw round it on ⅛ in. (3mm) thick wood. Using a ⅛ in. (3mm) drill bit, drill a hole at the end of each slot.

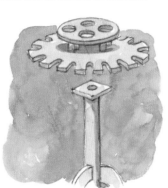

4 Cut a 2¼ in. (58mm) length of ⁵⁄₁₆ in. (8mm) round dowel. From ⅛ in. (3mm) wood, use the leg template (C) to cut three leg pieces. On the same wood draw out a ¾ in. (20mm) square. Drill a hole in the center using a ⁵⁄₁₆ in. (8mm) drill bit. Cut out the square.

2 With a jig or coping saw cut out the large circle. Extend the slots to the edge of the circle using a craft knife.

drinks table templates

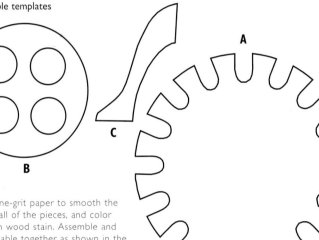

5 Use fine-grit paper to smooth the edges of all of the pieces, and color them with wood stain. Assemble and glue the table together as shown in the diagram. Add the bottle holder on top, supported by four legs cut from ⅛ in. (3mm) round dowel.

3 Follow steps one and two using template B, but do not make slots, just drill holes to hold the miniature wine bottles.

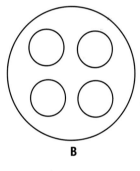

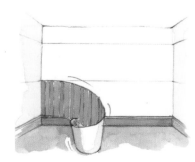

2 Measure the distances between the different lines. Cut a strip of striped wallpaper to fit between the skirting board and the chair rail line. Cover the back of the paper with a thin layer of wallpaper paste and stick it in place.

3 Cut strips of wallpaper and textured paper to fit in the areas above the chair and picture rails and glue them in place.

4 Cut lengths of narrow chair rail and picture rail to fit one wall. At the corners, cut the pieces into a 45-degree angle (a miter). This is best achieved using a small miter block. Any staining or painting should be completed before gluing the pieces in place.

PERIOD POINTS

• Use decorative repeat-pattern wallpapers to give a Victorian dining room its opulent and richly detailed effect. Lines of wooden molding, as wainscot and chair rails, and stained a deep mahogany brown, divide the walls into pleasing sections against which furniture can be displayed.

• Construct a formal dining table layout by preparing a white linen tablecloth, dipped in white glue to give it a lasting draped arrangement. Choose a fine porcelain dinner service on which to set out a satisfying supper.

• Choose fine items such as a mahogany display cabinet, a grandfather clock, and a fine plasterwork fireplace as the main features of this small yet impressive room, around which smaller items and accessories can be positioned.

The old curiosity shop

Include a gilded mirror for a hint of opulence.

The old curiosity shop is a nineteenth-century store displaying a medley of dollhouse items from different periods and styles. A miniature antiques store is an excellent place in which to display individual items and special pieces from your collection. Their presence adds intrigue and interest to such a treasure trove, waiting to be discovered by an enthusiastic collector. In an antiques store, a mixture of historical items can appear in the same scene, reflecting the enormous range of designs and styles available for dollhouse interior decorators. Prepare your store with as many shelving units, tables, and other surfaces—such as a broad window ledge—as possible, on which to stack and arrange tiny items of glassware and fine porcelain, fine items of garden statuary, and copper pots. Trays, boxes, and crates can also be used to store smaller items of curiosity, such as postcards, tools, kitchenware, and toys. In this chapter, find out how to make a range of projects that could appear in other rooms or period styles, or which could appear together in this fascinating old curiosity shop.

A brass light fitting provides an authentic period touch.

THE BASICS

▶ MAKING A FLOOR

The worn edges and color variations across the surface of the floorboards in this old curiosity shop show the wear and tear of many passing feet. Before laying floorboards on to your store floor, roughen each piece to achieve this worn look. Sand the boards, stain them, and then sand again unevenly. Score the surface with a knife, then stain and sand again. Repeat until a worn finish is achieved, and then lay the floorboards.

STAIRS

A flight of stairs can be installed at the back of the store leading to an upstairs room featuring more antiques and curiosities. Treat the wooden step pieces in the same way as the floorboards, staining and scoring the pieces to give the impression of wear and tear. Use a chisel to remove extra wood from the middle of each piece, where many feet have trod.

◀ BANISTERS

Ready-made banisters are available from dollhouse suppliers, and are often inexpensive, as they can be mass-produced on a copying lathe. In this setting, plain pine banisters (such as those shown on the left) can be combined with a dark hand rail and mounted between dark newel posts, to give an attractive contrasting effect.

FURNITURE AND FITTINGS

▶COT

This cot has a classic look that would suit any period of home. It could be passed down through the family, as a bed for generations of children. It would be suitable for interiors from the nineteenth century and earlier, especially those in which handmade furniture is a design feature. Instructions for making the cot are on page 91.

▼COPPERWARE

Burnished copper makes handsome items to stock in the old curiosity shop. Some can be sold as planters for large houseplants, such as aspidistra and ferns. Others would make attractive pots for a conservatory or kitchen. To encourage copper items to take on the patina of old age, leave them outside for a few weeks before placing them in your miniature store.

▶SIDE TABLE

A pretty little side table can be built from different colored woods, with panels of tiny scraps of colored paper arranged to look like marquetry. The legs are given a turned effect without the use of a lathe, by scribing lines into the sides of square-cut legs and trimming wood away to leave ridges and grooves. Instructions for making the side table are on page 90.

◀TIER SHELVES

These lightweight display shelves are called tier shelves or sometimes, rather quaintly, a "whatnot." They are ideally suited for a store setting, but would also fit in a domestic interior where they could hold a collection of prized ornaments. See page 90 for instructions on making the shelves.

▶ORGAN AND STOOL

An impressive piece of furniture, such as this musical organ, would wait for the perfect buyer to adopt it into his or her life. The organ probably came from a church, and has the worn look of an item that has seen many years of loyal service. On page 92 find out how to create a decorative little stool suitable as an organ or piano stool or as a bench in a dollhouse garden or conservatory.

▼TRAY OF PORCELAIN

A collection of porcelain, or a complete service of a particular design, can be stacked onto a tray for display as a set for sale to the highest bidder. Trim the top edge of a wooden tray into a wavy line for a decorative finish. To make the tray, glue strips of ⅛ in. (3mm) thick wood around the edge of a rectangle of the same wood. Varnish to finish.

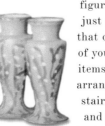

▶BOOKSHELVES AND BOOKS

Always useful, bookshelves are snapped up quickly from antiques stores by people who like to collect and display decorative items in their own homes. A simple design has a timeless appeal that would suit it to dollhouse rooms of many different periods. Choose wood with a fine grain for strength and to ensure that the sides and top will look attractive once varnished. Instructions for making the bookshelves are on page 93.

ADD TO THE LOOK

▶PICTURE FRAMES

Framed pictures and mirrors are essential items for any dollhouse interiors' enthusiast. The old curiosity shop displays many fine examples, demonstrating how small variations can adapt pictures to suit different periods of house. On page 92 you can find out how to make some of these different types of picture frame.

An old curiosity shop can be packed full of interesting items—fine china, glassware, figurines, books, pots, and furniture being just some of the miniature artifacts that could grace the shelves and tables of your own store. Seek out unusual items, and group them in attractive arrangements. Shelves fitted under the stairs will give extra display space, and some items can be hung on brass hooks screwed into the ceiling.

TIER SHELVES

This useful set of shelves is a delightful place to display many items, especially in a store setting. The open shelves offer a good view of displayed items from all sides, ideal for pots, silver cups, vases, decorative bowls, and small objets d'art. The uprights for these shelves are created from ready-made dollhouse banisters, with tiny wooden beads at the corner of each shelf to complete the effect.

❶ From ⅛ in. (3mm) thick wood, cut the following:
Top shelf: 1 piece, 1⅛ x 3 in. 29 x 76mm)
Second shelf: 1 piece, 1⅛ x 3½ in. (29 x 89mm)
Third shelf: 1 piece, 1⅛ x 4 in. (29 x 102mm)
Bottom shelf: 1 piece, 1⅛ x 4⁹⁄₁₆ in. (29 x 115mm)
From ⅛ in. (3mm) diameter ready-made dollhouse banisters cut 8 pieces, each 1³⁄₁₆ in. (30mm) long, and 4 pieces, each 1⅜ in. (35mm) long.

❷ Using a ¹⁄₁₆ in. (2mm) drill, make one hole in each corner of the top shelf. Make two holes in the corner of each of the remaining shelves, one ³⁄₁₆ in. (5mm) in from each edge, and the other ½ in. (12mm) in from the short edge and ³⁄₁₆ in. (5mm) in from the long edge.

❸ Trim a ¹⁄₁₆ in. (2mm) length at each end of each post to be slightly narrower. Lightly sand and stain all of the posts and shelves. Assemble and glue the posts and shelves together as shown in the diagram with the four longest posts at the lowest level.

❹ Glue matching ³⁄₁₆ in. (5mm) diameter beads at the top of each post, resting in the holes. Glue four shaped beads to the base as feet. Varnish to finish.

SIDE TABLE

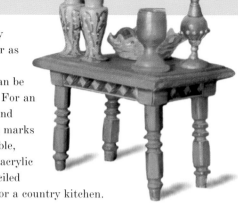

A side table is useful in many settings to carry tiny items or as a worktable for a child. The basic pattern for this table can be adapted to different periods. For an older table, use dark woods and score the surface to show the marks of long use. For a modern table, paint the finished piece with acrylic paint and decorate with stenciled motifs for a child's bedroom or a country kitchen.

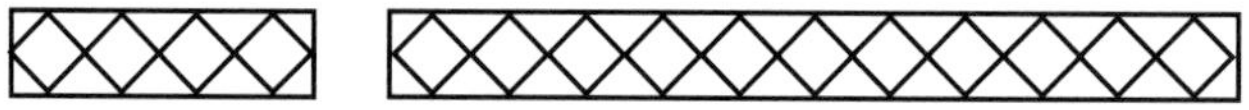

end layout guide   side layout guide

❶ From ⅛ in. (3mm) wood, cut the following:
Top: 1 piece, 1⅝ x 3 in. (41 x 76mm)
Sides: 2 pieces, each ¼ x 2¼ in. (6 x 58mm)
Ends: 2 pieces, each ¼ x ¾ in. (6 x 20mm)
From ¼ in. (6mm) square wood, cut 4 corner blocks, each ¼ in. (6mm) long
From ³⁄₁₆ in. (5mm) wood, cut 4 legs, each 1¼ in. (32mm) long
Lightly sand and stain all of the pieces. Stain the side and end pieces with dark mahogany stain.

❷ Cut 30 ⁵⁄₃₂ in. (4mm) squares of brown paper and decorate the side and end pieces with them, following the layout guides.

❸ Using a ¹⁄₁₆ in. (2mm) drill bit, drill a hole through each square corner block and into the top of each leg. Screw a leg to each block. Scribe lines into the sides of the legs and trim wood away to leave ridges and grooves.

❹ Glue the legs, side, and end pieces in place on the underside of the table. Varnish to finish.

COT

This attractive little cot has a homemade look, lovingly created by a proud father to hold a newborn child. The sturdy rockers set into the base allowed parents to rock their baby in a soothing motion, helping him or her to drop off to sleep. A handhold cut into the back face meant that the cot was easy to move, without disturbing the sleeping child.

DECORATING THE COT

A plain cot will suit a simple interior. For a more ornate finish, you can decorate the cot with a painted finish. For extra detail, glue a line of thin gold braid all the way around the top edge of the cot. Pretty additions can be a lace edge to a pillow and a soft satin coverlet in a pastel shade.

1 Copy the templates onto paper and cut them out. Draw round them on ⅛ in. (3mm) thick wood. Draw round the side and rocker pieces twice each. With a ¹⁄₁₆ in. (2mm) drill bit, make a hole at each end of the handhold. Use a sharp knife to remove the wood between the holes.

2 Cut out the pieces using a sharp knife or jig saw and sand the edges smooth. Stain all of the pieces. Assemble and glue the sides and ends together as shown in the diagram.

3 Cut slots in the base piece at the positions marked in gray on the pattern. Glue the rockers into the slots.

4 Position the base inside the cot, then use a knife to trim off any excess wood to help it fit neatly. Glue in position. Fill the cot with a folded square of blanket material. Tuck a piece of colored fabric over the top, and add a tiny pillow.

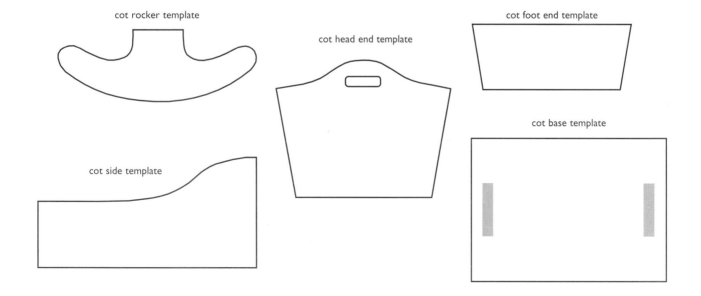

cot rocker template

cot head end template

cot foot end template

cot side template

cot base template

ORGAN STOOL

A well-made little organ stool would make a useful addition to a room containing a piano or organ. The seat is sloped to allow the musician to sit comfortably, his or her legs well out of the way of the keyboard, yet still able to operate the pedals. Choose a wood stain or paint to match the stool to your piano or organ. To adapt the stool as a garden or conservatory bench, follow the same instructions but trim the top of the leg pieces to give a flat surface and extend the length of the seat and rails.

MUSICAL MANUSCRIPT

Musical instruments such as an organ or a piano are an attractive addition to domestic interiors, hinting at a level of artistry and culture among the inhabitants of the dollhouse. Manuscript music can be added to such a scene by using a photocopier to reduce real sheet music down to dollhouse scale.

leg template

❶ From ⅛ in. (3mm) thick wood, cut the following:
Seat: 1¼ x 2⅙ in. (32 x 52mm)
Feet: 2 pieces, each ½ x 1 in. (12 x 25mm)

❷ Trace and cut out the leg template. Draw round the shape twice on ⅛ in. (3mm) thick wood, flipping the paper template for the second piece. Following the pattern, with a ¹⁄₁₆ in. (2mm) drill bit, make five holes in each piece at the positions marked in black, and two holes in each piece, halfway through the wood, at the positions marked in gray.

❸ Cut two 1½ in. (38mm) lengths of ⅛ in. (3mm) diameter ready-made dollhouse banisters. Trim a ¹⁄₁₆ in. (2mm) length at each end of each post to be slightly narrower.

❹ Lightly sand and stain all of the stool pieces, then assemble and glue them together as shown in the diagram. Varnish to finish.

PICTURE FRAMES

Different styles of picture frame can be created using the same basic technique, for which instructions are provided here. For an ornate frame, glue on shaped jewelry fittings before painting the frame gold. For a plain frame, use textured molding, or varnish a simple wood frame and add brass-effect corners. Frame pictures cut from art catalogs, greeting cards, or family photographs.

❶ Prepare the picture by gluing it to a rectangle of cardboard, with a ¼ in. (6mm) border around the edge.

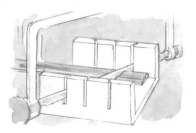

❷ Cut lengths of ¼ in. (6mm) wooden molding, using both the length and the height of the picture as your internal measurements for the frame. Cut the ends at a 45-degree angle, using a miter block.

BOOKSHELVES

Most dollhouse rooms will benefit from a set of low-level bookshelves, providing a place to store books and papers, with an extra surface on which to display a lamp and ornaments. You can adapt the template and measurements to fit your own miniature book collection, or add extra shelves to accommodate smaller items. For an ornate finish to the side panels, you could carve geometric patterns framed by a rectangle of thin wood strips cut into miters at the corners. Use a craft knife to scribe lines before staining and varnishing the piece.

side template

❶ From ⅛ in. (3mm) thick wood, cut the following:
Sides: 2 pieces, each ¾ × 2½ in. (20 × 64mm)
Base and top: 2 pieces, each 1 × 2¹⁄₁₆ in. (25 × 52mm)
Shelves: 2 pieces, each ¾ × 1¾ in. (20 × 44mm)
From ¹⁄₃₂ in. (1mm) thick wood, cut 1 back piece, 1¹³⁄₁₆ × 2½ in. (47 × 64mm)
Lightly sand and stain all of the pieces.

❷ Cut slots in the side pieces in the positions marked in gray on the template. Cut halfway through the wood.

❸ Cut a ¹⁄₁₆ in. (2mm) square from each corner of each shelf. Assemble and glue the shelves together as shown in the diagram. You may have to adjust the shelf tongues slightly to fit. Glue the back piece in place. Sand and varnish to finish.

CHILDREN'S SHELVES

A set of simple bookshelves would make a useful addition to a child's playroom or bedroom, for storing books and toys. Paint the finished shelves in primary or pastel color. Add paintings of teddy bears or balloons, or cut tiny pictures from children's toy catalogs and glue them to the shelves as decoupage. In either case, finish with acrylic varnish.

❸ Glue the pieces together into a frame, sand any rough edges, and then decorate the frame in the style of your choice:
For a textured frame, place the end of a metal bar on the wood and tap it lightly with a hammer to make an indent. Repeat around the frame.
For a frame with decorative motifs, glue tiny jewelry fittings to the frame.
For a frame with brass fittings, varnish the plain, wood frame and then glue strips of cardboard around the corners.

❹ Color the textured and decorated frames with gold metallic spray paint. For the plain frame with brass corners, color only the cardboard corners with gold metallic spray paint. When dry, glue the picture to the back. Attach a hanging hook, such as a dressmaker's hook from a hook-and-eye set. Alternatively, screw a tiny screw-eye into each side of the frame and attach a hanging thread.

Frank Lloyd Wright
sitting room

One of the greatest architects working in the first half of the twentieth century was Frank Lloyd Wright, who sought to create a harmony between the external structure and the interior design of the houses and public buildings that he designed. This beautiful sitting room, a copy of a room in Grand Rapids, Michigan, uses tall windows and skylights to invite the sunshine into the room and create elegant frames through which to view the garden. Wright thought of his architecture as music. "A building should resemble a symphony," he said, "an edifice of sound." The musical metaphor is expressed in this room in the designs and colors chosen to unify the furniture, textiles, and jewel-like stained glass. The mirror, window, skylights, wall light, embroidery, and armchairs all carry echoes of a grid-like geometric pattern that in its turn complements the intricate structure of the window frames. Each repetition is like a musician returning to and embellishing a musical theme.

In this chapter you will find out how to capture the essence of Frank Lloyd Wright's work, using the natural materials and colors that this inspiring architect so valued.

A highly polished desk is an elegant addition to this stylish sitting room.

Create colorful sunflowers from scraps of card to display in a sunny window.

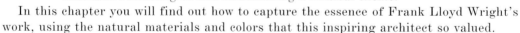

THE BASICS

◄ MAKING A FLOOR

Natural materials are an important feature of Frank Lloyd Wright's work. Dollhouse paper flooring can give the effect of fine wooden parquet, on which to display the embroidered rug featured on page 101. Or line the whole floor with a fine-grain wood such as maple or oak. Finish a wooden floor with several coats of varnish.

◄ THE WALLS

Sturdy pillars standing between the floor-to-ceiling windows create a monumental feel to the room. This structure helps to give the room a sense of solidity whilst letting in a flood of light. Choose from a range of autumnal colors, described by Wright as the "optimistic tones of earth and autumn leaves," to line the walls with smooth cardboard—a rich background for the wooden detail.

◄ WINDOWS

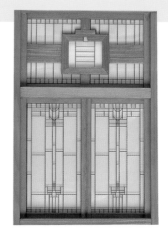

Framed by lengths of wood strip, the windows are built up piece by piece to create the impressive design that frames large panels of stained glass. In this miniature scene, the stained glass has been created on sheets of plastic—the details added with a permanent marker, and the colored areas with glass paints or colored permanent felt-tip pens. Instructions on page 100 will help you recreate this effect in your own dollhouse.

FURNITURE AND FITTINGS

◀ARMCHAIR

The repeated upright lines of the window are reflected in the design of the armchair with its grid of bars at each side. A section of the stained-glass window design is also picked out in embroidery on the cushion, making the chair an integral part of the room.

▶CABINET

The framed panels of the walls are echoed on the front of this useful little cabinet, set in an attractive sunny alcove, making it the perfect piece of furniture to carry a vase of flowers. The gold handle is a single ring cut from a necklace—imitating the fine-quality fittings that Wright insisted upon using.

▶RUG

"It is quite impossible," said Wright, "to consider the building as one thing and its furnishings another." Even the rugs in this harmonized room were designed by Wright himself, with the motifs echoing the grid, diagonals, and splashes of color in the stained-glass windows. Instructions for creating this rug are on page 101.

▲DESK

Set in a pool of natural light, the beautiful polished wooden top of this desk, and the sculptural objects on it, are shown off to their best advantage. The instructions on page 99 take you through the steps to recreate this desk, made simply from panels and blocks glued together and finished with a line of molding around the base.

▲LAMP

The effect of light coming through colored glass was a favorite theme of Frank Lloyd Wright. A Tiffany-style lamp is the perfect addition to this scene, bringing a warm glow of color as the evening draws in and creating a focal point for the room. There are many fine examples available from specialist dollhouse suppliers.

▶SKYLIGHT

The room thrusts outwards into the garden, with a tiled walkway outside. The design of the roof makes good use of this opportunity to let in more light through a set of skylights. Each skylight is a frame of wood strip, displaying a beautiful panel of stained glass.

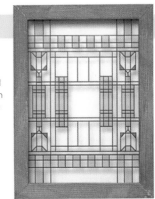

▶TEXTILES

Choose textiles and yarns that echo the colors of the stained glass. Cut rectangles of coarse-weave orange linen to protect the polished surfaces of the furniture. If you take care to cut along the lines of the weave, and remove a few threads on each side, then there is no need to hem them.

▶MIRROR

An element of the window's stained-glass design is repeated as the motif on this elegant mirror. Created quite simply by adding a strip of thin plastic to the surface of the mirror glass, the design is drawn out with permanent felt-tip pens (see page 99).

ADD TO THE LOOK

▶LIGHTING

Simple wall lights, fitted according to the manufacturer's instructions, can be adapted to fit the style of the room by the addition of a tracing-paper covering, marked out with a grid-like motif and mounted on strips of wood. Make sure that the paper is far enough away from the bulb not to get singed.

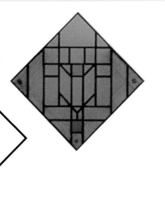

On the desk, boxes can be used to display dried grasses or store pencils made from lengths cut from painted wooden toothpicks. A display of paper flowers adds a lively splash of color to the room. The sunflowers on page 96 were cut from yellow paper, trimmed to form petals. A circle of felt in the center makes the seed head, and a length of green garden wire glued to the back creates the stem. Display them in a tiny pot with paper leaves cut from green paper.

CHAIR

With its low seat, wooden arms, and high, cushioned back, this comfortable chair is based on a design that appeared many times in interiors crafted by Frank Lloyd Wright over the course of his long career. A grid of bars along each side and embroidered cushions tailor the chair to fit with this room, but the tried-and-tested shape is a classic Wright design.

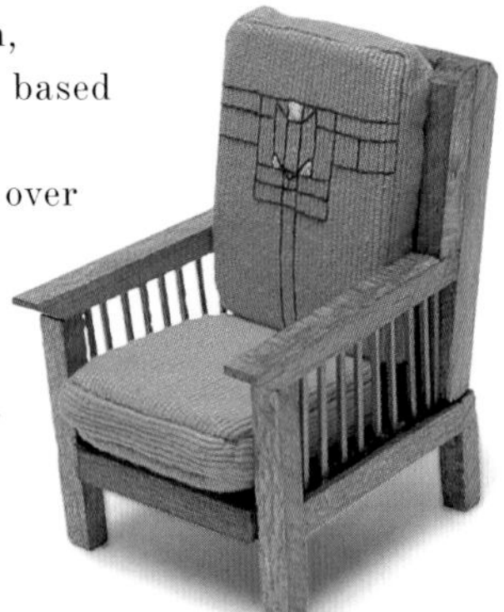

❶ From ¼ in. (6mm) thick wood, cut the following:
Arms: 2 pieces, each ¼ in. (6mm) x 2⅝ in. (67mm)
Seat: 1 piece, 2⅝ in. (67mm) x 2½ in. (64mm). From each corner, remove a ¼ in. (6mm) square.
Back: 1 piece, 2½ in. (64mm) x 2¾ in. (70mm)
Back legs: 2 pieces, each ¼ in. (6mm) x 1¹⁄₁₆ in. (28mm)
Front legs: 2 pieces, each ¼ in. (6mm) x 2¹⁄₁₆ in. (52mm)
Backrest sides: 2 pieces, each ¼ in. (6mm) x 1½ in. (38mm)
From ¹⁄₁₆ in. (2mm) square wood strip, cut 18 bars, each 1¼ in. (32mm) long.
Lightly sand, then stain all of the pieces.

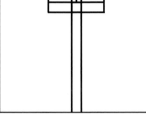
embroidery layout guide

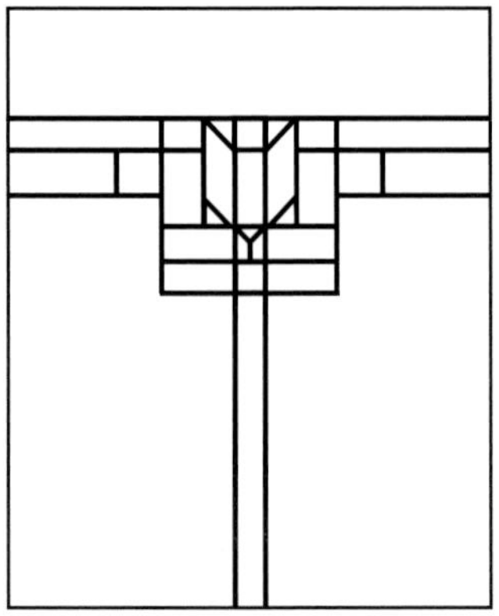

❷ Use a knife to cut a ¼ in. (6mm) long wedge from under the front of each arm, using the photograph as a guide. On the underside of each arm, score two lines, and chisel out a ¹⁄₁₆ in. (2mm) wide, ¹⁄₁₆ in. (2mm) deep trench. Make similar trenches on the long sides of the seat piece.

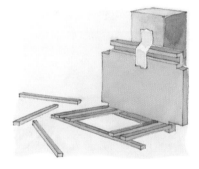

❸ Run a little glue along one trench on the seat piece. Tape the seat to a box or tin so that it stands upright. Push nine of the bars into the glue, with regular spaces in between. Support the loose ends on a ⅛ in. (3mm) strip of wood. When dry, assemble the other side in the same way.

❹ Round off the top edges of the back and backrest sides with sandpaper. The back end of each arm piece, and the bottoms of the back piece and backrest sides should be trimmed to a slight angle to give a comfortable angle to the chair.

❺ Assemble and glue the chair pieces together as shown in the diagram. Varnish to finish.

UPHOLSTERED CUSHION

❶ For the upright cushion, cut the following:
Two rectangles of cardboard, each 1¾ in. (45mm) x 2⅜ in. (60mm)
Two rectangles of fabric, each 2¼ in. (57mm) x 2⅞ in. (73mm)
One rectangle of fabric, ⅞ in. (22mm) x 8 in. (203mm)
For the seat cushion, cut the following:
Two rectangles of cardboard, each 1¾ in. (45mm) x 2 in. (50mm)
Two rectangles of fabric, each 2¼ in. (57mm) x 2½ in. (64mm)
One rectangle of fabric, ⅞ in. (22mm) x 7¼ in. (185mm)

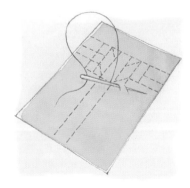

❷ Upright cushion: Use the layout guide to sew lines of black stitching in a geometric pattern on one of the large pieces of fabric. Follow the lines of the weave to keep the design regular. Embroider a few stitches of yellow to highlight the square and triangles.

❸ Make both cushions in the same way. Use matching thread to sew the long strip around three edges of a rectangle leaving a ¼ (6mm) seam allowance. Sew the other rectangle to the other side of the strip. Turn the cushion right side out; insert the two pieces of cardboard, one lying next to each fabric side.

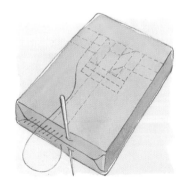

❹ Fill the middle with a little stuffing, foam, or with scraps of fabric. Push the raw edges of fabric inside and stitch the hole closed.

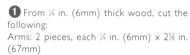

DESK

The shapes and style of the room are reflected in the construction of this impressive desk. A thrusting section at the front echoes the pillars in the room, and strips of wood make a frame on the front that echoes the paneling on the walls. It is given a stylish finish with molding strips around the base.

1 From 3/16 in. (5mm) thick wood, cut the following:
Front: One piece, 2⅜ in. (60mm) x 4 in. (102mm)
Sides: Two pieces, each 2⅜ in. (60mm) x 1½ in. (38mm)
Drawer panels: Two pieces, each 2⅜ in. (60mm) x 1½ in. (38mm)
Thrust front: One piece, 2⅜ in. (60mm) x 1½ in. (38mm)
Thrust sides: Two pieces, each 2⅜ in. (60mm) x ⅜ in. (10mm)

Top: One piece, 2½ in. (64mm) x 5 in. (125mm)
From ½ in. (12mm) square wood, cut four internal supports, each 2⅜ in. (60mm) long
From 1/16 in. (2mm) thick wood, cut four drawer fronts, each ⅝ in. (16mm) x 1 1/16 in. (27mm)
Sand and stain all of the pieces.
NB. See page 97 for a picture of the front of the desk.

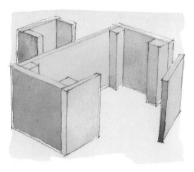

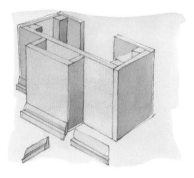

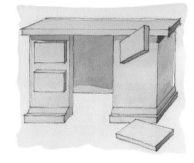

2 Assemble and glue the main box as shown, gluing the supports inside the corners. Assemble and glue the thrust pieces, and stick to the front of the desk.

3 Cut strips of molding with mitered corners to fit around the base of the desk. Stain the pieces, then glue them in place. Glue the top of the desk in place.

4 From 1/32 in. (1mm) thick wood, cut tiny, mitered strips to create a frame on the front of the thrust section. Stain the pieces, then glue them in place.

5 Glue the drawer fronts to the drawer panels. Varnish the whole desk. When dry, glue a small ring (cut from a necklace) to each drawer front.

MIRROR

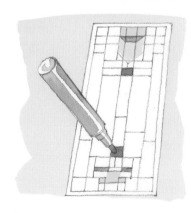

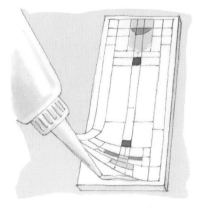

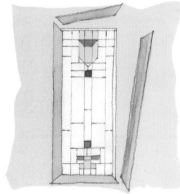

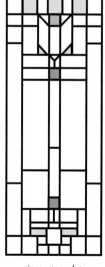

An elegant mirror becomes an integral part of this setting by the addition of a geometric design.

1 Cut a piece of clear stiff plastic, 1½ in. (38mm) x 3⅛ in. (80mm) (plastic from food packaging is suitable). Tape it over the layout design and trace the pattern using a black permanent felt-tip pen (see instructions for window). Remove the tape and use orange and yellow permanent felt-tip pens to color the squares and triangles.

2 Cut a piece of mirror cardboard or plastic mirror tile, 1½ in. (38mm) x 3⅛ in. (80mm). Glue the plastic design on top (pen side down), attaching it with a very thin line of white glue around the edge.

3 Frame the mirror with strips of ¼ in. (6mm) wide wooden molding, with miter corners. Stain the pieces before gluing them in place. Glue or tape a hanging thread on the back of the frame.

mirror template

ART-GLASS WINDOW

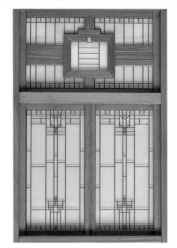

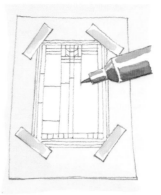

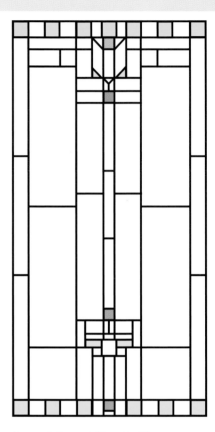

Stained glass or "art glass" with complex geometric patterns is a hallmark of Frank Lloyd Wright's work. Every view in the building incorporates glimpses of glowing glass colors—giving a rich texture to the light in the rooms and hallways. You can fit panels to existing windows to give a stained-glass effect by removing the glass, inserting a patterned piece of plastic, then refitting the glass to hold it in place.

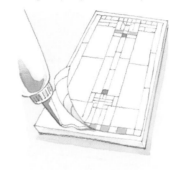

❶ Remove one of the windows from your dollhouse. Take it apart and cut a piece of clear, stiff plastic the same size as the glass (Perspex is suitable).

❷ Tape the plastic over the layout guide and trace the pattern using black marker pen. If you are working on a small window, trace part of the design onto the plastic. Remove the tape and use orange and yellow permanent felt-tip pens to color the squares and triangles, as indicated in the layout guide.

❸ Glue the plastic to the glass with tiny dabs of PVA glue (that will be transparent when dry), as shown on the left. When dry, reassemble the window.

lower window panel layout guide

PLANTS

Frank Lloyd Wright's love of nature meant that special places for plants were often incorporated into his architectural designs. One house, built in River Forest, Illinois, even incorporated a living tree as part of the hipped roof of the porch. It is still growing and thriving nearly 100 years later.

In this room, a pot of sunflowers is shown off in a broad sunny alcove. Large plants are displayed in pots that carry geometric designs to reflect the motifs of the décor, bringing a touch of nature into this sunny interior and giving the room the feel of a conservatory. The pot for this plant was made from polymer clay and scribed with a geometric design before baking.

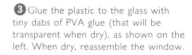

❶ For a large fern, glue the ends of four lengths of dark green pipe cleaner into a pot.

RUG

1 For a 5½ in. (140mm) x 6¾ in. (171mm) rug, use canvas with 16 holes per inch (25mm). Cut a piece of canvas 6½ in. (165mm) x 7¾ in. (197mm). Choose yarns that complement each other—such as gray, white, ginger, yellow, and green, and scraps of orange and purple. Try to use colors that already appear in the room—such as the orange of the chair cushions.

stitching guide

Frank Lloyd Wright's interiors are characterized by great attention to detail. Furniture, fittings, textiles, and stained glass all echo the same patterns, adapted to suit the particular materials. The repeated lines and long thin rectangles of this canvas-work rug are no exception—even the splashes of orange and green are carefully selected to chime with other elements of the room's decor.

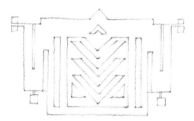

2 Using the stitching guide, copy the design onto the canvas. Each square represents one diagonal stitch. Ideally, mount the canvas on an embroidery frame to keep it in shape. Start with gray yarn and map out the main lines of the design.

3 Start each new piece of yarn with a knot in one end. Add the white, orange, ginger, green and purple areas. Use yellow yarn to stitch the background. Extend the background by as many extra lines of yellow as you wish.

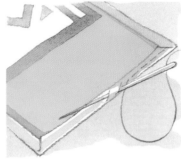

4 When complete, if the piece has got out of shape, wet it and pin it out on a board, stretching it back into a rectangle. When dry, fold the edges underneath and hold them in place with stitches of sewing thread.

2 Cut leaves from dark green cardboard, trimming the edges into pointed fringe shapes. Glue them together in threes and then to the ends of the pipe cleaners. Finish the leaves with clear acrylic varnish.

3 For a cheese plant, press a single pipe cleaner into a blob of air-drying modeling clay and push this into a pot.

4 Cut cheese-plant leaf shapes from green cardboard, using the photograph as a guide. Score each leaf down the middle using the end of a blunt stick.

5 Glue a narrow strip of cardboard to the back of each leaf, and glue the other ends to the pipe cleaner. Finish the leaves with clear acrylic varnish.

An elegant display cabinet for a collection of fine ornaments.

1920s
living room

What better place to spend an evening than in a pleasant living room complete with a cozy fire, a writing desk, and a grand piano? This room, furnished in the early part of the twentieth century, is from an educated lady's residence. It is fitted out for gentle pursuits, such as reading, music-making, writing, and polite conversation. Evidently designed for a woman of some means, the furnishings and accessories are of high quality. Textiles line the walls, and fine drapes grace the windows. A well-crafted screen is ornamented with beautifully mounted sepia photographs of relatives. Elegant furniture is unified into a single designed set with symmetrical flourishes and the choice of a fine golden wood. In this chapter, you can discover the tools and techniques to help you create some of the classic items from this attractive little scene—from a fretwork display cabinet to a leather-bound writing set.

A set of novels or study books can be moved to another room in the house in this attractive book carrier.

THE BASICS

MAKING A FLOOR
A wooden floor can be given an elegant finishing touch with a geometric border. This effect is created with three strips of thin brown cardboard. With a craft knife cut the middle strip into a lattice pattern that echoes the lozenge design on the display cabinet. Use the layout guide, *right*. Glue the pieces around the edge of the floor, then varnish to finish.

THE WALLS
Embroidered fabric makes a delightful wall covering against which fine portraits can be displayed. This satin fabric, with a formal woven design, has been mounted onto rectangles of cardboard, attached to the wall and framed with strips of wood. Follow instructions on page 107 to achieve this effect in your own dollhouse room.

CHOOSING A WOOD
The welcoming effect of this room is created by the choice of a warm-colored wood for the walls, floor, and skirting board. This gives an overall harmonious look well suited to the period. Furniture has been carefully chosen to match the choice of wood.

floor border layout guide

FURNITURE AND FITTINGS

◀ DESK

A practical little desk combines a number of functions in one piece of furniture. Drawers provide storage space, and the top section folds out to provide a spacious counter. A panel of arches at the back of the desk holds all types of correspondence—letters from friends and family, as well as bills and legal documents. The top surface provides the perfect place for a telephone. Instructions for the desk are on page 106.

◀ DISPLAY CABINET

This elegant display cabinet is an impressive piece of furniture with its carved top section and its delicate tracery on the glass panel doors. It is a perfect place to display a collection of fine ornaments, such as porcelain figurines or delicate glassware. The tracery, with its lozenge shapes, is echoed in the patterning of the parquet floor. Adapt a ready-made glass-fronted cabinet by the addition of a top piece and tracery cut from thick cardboard and painted to match the wood. Instructions are on page 108.

▲ CHAIR

A sturdy wooden chair is suitable for a lady sitting down to work at her desk. The armchairs that also feature in this scene are intended for leisure moments, but this upright chair is for times when the occupant needs to be more busy and alert. A single cushion is the only concession to comfort. Instructions for the chair are on page 107.

FIREPLACE

An intricate plasterwork fireplace makes a focal point for the room, and many attractive examples are available from dollhouse suppliers. In front of the fireplace, fit an area of dark wood as a hearth, painted gray to look like stone. Frame the hearth with strips of wooden molding.

▶ SCREEN

On long winter evenings, even a well-laid fire would not be sufficient to keep the lady of the house warm as she sat composing letters, practicing her music at the piano, or putting the finishing touches to a piece of embroidery. A screen served to cut down on draughts from the window and to reflect the fire's heat back into the room. A template and instructions for making this folding screen are provided on page 109.

◀ PORTRAIT

Fine portraits in gold frames adorn the walls of this room. Black-and-white etchings of literary and historical figures reflect the interests of the lady of the house. From gold cardboard cut out an oval shape for a mount. Glue a tiny portrait to the back of the mount. Frame with wood strip, painted gold.

◀ FLORAL DISPLAY

This cozy little house would probably have a cottage garden full of beautiful plants and flowers which would make lovely floral decorations to brighten up the room, such as this basket containing a pretty single rose bloom. To find out how to create a rose in a basket from colored tissue paper, see the instructions on page 106.

◀ VASE STAND

A large Chinese porcelain vase is a beautiful ornament to grace a corner of this elegant room. A good stand on which to display the piece can be made from a dark wooden dollhouse bowl with small wooden feet glued to the base. Cover the top with a circle of thin wood and paint it to match the bowl.

ADD TO THE LOOK

THE MIRROR

A fine mirror is mounted above the fireplace. In front of it, a clock and porcelain vases are displayed on the mantelpiece. Two glass candlesticks complete the look. Frame a small mirror with wooden molding with mitered corners. Paint the frame white and pick out the details with gold metallic paint.

A lady of leisure would take great pleasure in sitting down to compose a letter to a close friend, lovingly written by hand. A stack of letters can be stored in the writing desk, tied together with embroidery floss. Recreate this attractive writing set for your own dollhouse following the instructions on page 109.

DESK

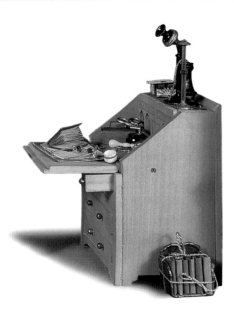

A writing desk can be adapted from a low chest of drawers by the addition of side pieces and a hinged lid. Inside, store bundles of letters tied together with embroidery floss, along with pens and a large blotting pad. See page 109 for instructions on how to make these items. On top of the desk you could place a pedestal telephone and a notepad for taking messages.

1 Trim a ⅛ in. (3mm) strip from the top of a chest of drawers. The top drawer will become the support for the open desk lid. Cut a rectangle of ⅛ in. (3mm) thick wood the same size as the back of the chest of drawers, plus an extra 1 in. (25mm) at the top. Sand and stain, and glue in position.

2 From ⅛ in. (3mm) thick wood, cut two side pieces to cover the side rectangles of the chest of drawers, extending above the top surface by 1 in. (25mm). Cut the front corner from each piece in an angle, leaving a ½ in. (12mm) section at the back uncut. Sand and stain.

3 From ⅛ in. (3mm) thick wood, for a top shelf, cut a rectangle ³⁄₁₆ in. (5mm) wider than the desk (with side pieces) and ½ in. (12mm) wide. Cut a mail-slot piece, 1 in. (25mm) tall and as wide as the gap between the two side pieces. Cut slots using the layout guide, then sand and stain. Glue in place at the back of the desk and glue the top shelf on top.

4 From ⅛ in. (3mm) thick wood, for the desk lid, cut a rectangle as wide as the gap between the two side pieces and as long as the distance between the front edge of the desk and the top edge of the mail-slot piece. Sand and stain. Attach the lid with two pins pushed in through the sides of the desk and into the bottom corners of the lid piece. You may need to drill tiny holes first, and round off the bottom edge of the lid with sandpaper to help it turn smoothly.

5 Glue a strip of wood at the top of the mail-slot piece to support the desk lid when shut. Attach a brass handle or bead to the front of the desk lid.

SUPPORTING THE DESK LID

When folded down, the desk lid should be held up by the front edge of the original chest of drawers. If this is not sufficient, pulling out the top drawer of the chest of drawers may provide more support. Or glue two slim blocks to the front of the desk similar to those in the picture.

internal mail slots layout guide

FABRIC WALL PANELS

At first, an onlooker might think the wall is lined with standard wallpaper. But closer inspection shows that the walls have a beautiful sheen achieved by the use of fine fabric mounted onto cardboard panels and framed with wooden molding. Pale motifs on a silver-gray satin background give a fascinating and subtle effect. Woven brocade fabrics in a single color would also be suitable. For the best effect, choose fabrics with a design small enough to repeat frequently across the wall.

1 Cut a large piece of thick cardboard, ¾ in. (20mm) smaller all round than the wall area to be covered.

2 Cut a piece of fabric larger than the cardboard by ½ in. (12mm) at each edge. Lay it out on a flat surface. Spray the cardboard with spray glue (sometimes sold as photograph mounting spray), and then lay it on top of the fabric. Gently smooth the fabric over the cardboard without stretching it.

3 When the glue is dry, fold the corners of the fabric over to the back of the cardboard and secure with white glue. Fold the edges of the fabric over and secure in the same way.

4 Glue the panels in position on the walls. Frame with lengths of stained wooden molding, cut into miters at the corners.

CHAIR

Correspondence was not to be lingered over, so a plain chair with a simple cushion offered sufficient comfort for the writer. For longer letters that needed careful thought, the lady might wander over to the more comfortable upholstered chairs and sofa by the fire. A small touch of decoration in the form of a shaped diamond pattern on the back of the chair is the only ornament on this practical piece of furniture.

1 From ³⁄₁₆ in. (5mm) square wood, cut the following:
Front legs: 2 pieces, each 2¼ in. (58mm) long
Back legs: 2 pieces, each 1⁷⁄₁₆ in. (37mm) long
Arms: 2 pieces, each 1⅜ in. (35mm) long
Front strut: 1 piece, 1³⁄₁₆ in. (30mm) long
From ³⁄₁₆ in. (5mm) thick wood, cut the following:
Base: 1 piece, 1⁹⁄₁₆ in. (40mm) square. Cut a ³⁄₁₆ in. (5mm) square from each corner. Lightly sand and stain all of the pieces.

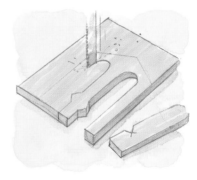

2 Copy the chair-back template onto paper and cut out. Use a sharp knife to cut out detailed areas. Draw round it on ³⁄₁₆ in. (5mm) thick wood and use a coping saw or jig saw to cut it. Sand and stain.

chair back template

3 Assemble and glue the pieces together as shown in the diagram. Varnish to finish.

DISPLAY CABINET

Collecting porcelain ornaments and figurines was an important pastime for the lady of this household. Her extensive collection is displayed in a large glass-fronted cabinet and a smaller one that evidently comes from the same set because they both have lozenge-shaped fretwork panels. You can add a fretwork design to a ready-made plain cabinet in the form of a cut cardboard lattice, painted to match the wood.

❶ Trace the door grid layout guide onto paper. For a smaller door, trim the design to make it smaller. For a larger door, extend the lines of the design at the top, bottom, and sides to fit your own display cabinet.

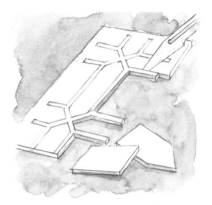

❷ Glue the paper to the back of a ⅟₁₆ in. (2mm) thick piece of cardboard. Carefully cut out the pattern, using a sharp craft knife.

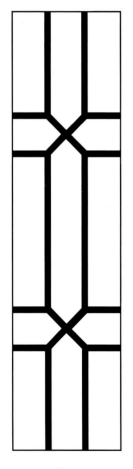

❸ Glue the fretwork to the cabinet glass, using tiny dabs of white glue. Paint the fretwork to match the cabinet. Varnish to finish.

❹ Copy the cabinet top curls template onto paper and cut it out. Draw round it on ⅟₁₆ in. (2mm) thick cardboard and cut it out. Trim the piece to suit the width of your cabinet. Glue the cardboard to the top of the cabinet, holding it upright with a short strip of wood glued behind the base. Paint it to match the cabinet.

CREATING A SET OF FURNITURE

• Make a coordinated set of display cabinets by adding the same fretwork design to the doors of different pieces of furniture. Use a photocopier to enlarge or reduce the door grid layout guide and the top curls template.

• Fretwork panels can also be added to the wooden sides of plain furniture such as a bookshelf, framed with strips of cardboard or wood and then painted and varnished to match.

• Add matching door handles to each piece of furniture with brass-effect beads, or specialist fittings purchased from a dollhouse supplier.

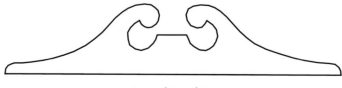

top curls template

door grid layout guide

FOLDING SCREEN

This unusual screen, with its undulating top, is easy to create from lengths of wood, with the minimum of shaping or carving. Three panels are joined together with ready-made dollhouse brass hinges. The smooth surfaces of the screen can be left plain, covered with panels of fabric, or decorated with simple stenciled paintings on floral themes. Alternatively, you could hang tiny framed photographs on tacks, as shown in the main picture.

WRITING SET

Although telephones were becoming popular among middle-class households in the first decades of the twentieth century, writing remained the most important means of keeping in touch—both for business and personal matters. So a practical desk at which to work was an important feature of an independent woman's house, as was a good set of writing equipment. This large blotter and dip pen are two items you would expect to find in a middle-class household.

❶ From ³⁄₁₆ in. (5mm) square wood cut the following:
Section 1: 1 piece, 3¹¹⁄₁₆ in. (94mm) long, and 1 piece, 4⅜ in. (111 mm) long
Section 2: 1 piece, 4⅜ in. (111mm) long, and 1 piece, 5¹⁄₁₆ in. (128mm) long
Section 3: 1 piece, 5¹⁄₁₆ in. (128mm) long, and 1 piece, 5¾ in. (145mm) long
From ³⁄₁₆ in. (5mm) thick wood, cut the following:
Section 1: 1 piece, 1¼ × 2½ in. (32 × 64mm)
Section 2: 1 piece, 1¼ × 3³⁄₁₆ in. (32 × 81mm)
Section 3: 1 piece, 1¼ × 3⅞ in. (32 × 98mm)
Lightly sand and stain all of the pieces.

❷ Copy the top curve template onto paper and cut it out. Draw round it three times on ³⁄₁₆ in. (5mm) thick wood. Use a jig saw to cut the pieces out. Sand and stain each piece.

❶ Cut one rectangle of watercolor paper, and one rectangle of cardboard larger than the watercolor paper by ¹⁄₁₆ in. (2mm) all round. Cover the cardboard with leather-effect green paper.

❷ Glue the watercolor paper on top. Glue a triangle of green leather-effect paper to each corner.

❸ Assemble and glue each screen section as shown in the diagram.

❹ Attach four hinges to Section 2, then attach the other two sections of the screen. Fold up the screen and rub the bases of the legs on sandpaper to help it stand flat. Hinges can be attached to give a zigzag or a curved folding screen, as indicated in the smaller diagrams above.

❸ Write a tiny letter with a black pen, and then reduce it with a photocopier to dollhouse size. Make envelopes in the same way, stack a few and tie them together with embroidery floss.

❹ For a pen, use a sharp craft knife to trim a length of wooden skewer into a nib shape. Scribe a line around the base of the nib, and then whittle the wood away to make a tapering handle. Paint the handle with acrylic paint and the nib with silver metallic paint. Add a tiny dot of black as an ink reservoir on the nib.

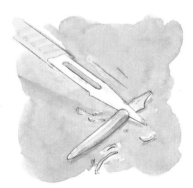

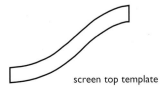

screen top template

American diner

Condiments and napkin dispensers add to the look.

Anyone old enough to have visited a 1950s' diner during his or her youth will remember with great nostalgia the sounds, smells, and atmosphere of this unique style of restaurant. The precursors of fast-food chains run by international companies, diners were often established by families working hard for long hours to create a welcoming, satisfying eating experience. Diners were set up in converted trailers and outbuildings alongside roads, and often used eye-catching signs on the roof—sometimes using symbols such as huge painted burgers or ice-cream sundaes, or simple statements such as "Eat" or "Food." These were designed to be spotted by passing drivers, tempting them to pull over, take a break, and enjoy the wonderful breakfasts, desserts, and hot drinks on offer. Customers became regulars, getting to know the owners and enjoying the feeling of a quiet welcome in familiar surroundings. In this chapter you will learn how to create the characteristic features of a 1950s' American diner using everyday materials and tools.

A porcelain replica of a 1950s' Wurlitzer jukebox.

THE BASICS

◄ MAKING A FLOOR

The diner floor is designed to be both attractive and easy to clean. Tiles were a popular choice, often plain black and white in a checkerboard design, or decorated with geometric patterns to bring color to the diner design. Tile paper is available from most dollhouse suppliers. This tiled floor, with tessellated triangles and squares, was created using a computer and a color printer. Alternatively, you can create tiles with accurately cut squares of shiny cardboard glued in a regular pattern across the floor.

◄ CHROME EDGING

A shiny chrome finish is an instantly recognizable feature of a 1950s' American diner. The edgings to the diner tables, the bar, and the raised platform underneath the jukebox are all created with narrow aluminum strip, available from an architectural modeling store. The table and bar top are made from thick poly-board, and the aluminum strip gives the surfaces the impression of solidity and period style.

► THE WALLS

Diners were often built inside steel trailers, so needed to be clad inside with wood or leather-effect vinyl panels to give them a warm and welcoming interior. This diner has red walls lined with leather-effect plasticized fabric, divided into panels with strips of stained wood and chrome bars. The chrome bars above the door are made with three lengths of wooden dowel glued together and sprayed with silver metallic paint. The steel exterior of the building is visible in the materials used for the window frames.

FURNITURE AND FITTINGS

▲ BAR
A tall bar is the central feature of an American diner, edged with aluminum strip and finished with a metal foot-rail held up by circular brackets. Each element can be recreated in miniature using modern materials, such as poly-board, aluminum strip and silver metallic spray paint. Instructions are on page 114.

▶ BAR STOOL
Solitary diners can enjoy a quiet moment eating breakfast and reading the newspaper perched on a bar stool and leaning on the bar. These stools have leather-effect plasticized fabric seats, firmly stuffed, with chrome fittings created from key-ring parts and lengths of wooden dowel sprayed silver. Instructions are on page 115.

▲ DINING TABLE
Modern poly-board is the ideal base for constructing this dining table. Covered in a textured paper to suggest a plasticized surface, it is edged with a narrow aluminum strip to complete the classic 1950s' look. The fixed legs are made from thick wooden dowel seated in wooden buttons, glued together and sprayed with metallic silver paint.

▲ GLASS SHELVES
Lit from above, these glass shelves display the glassware of the busy diner. The shelves are created from strips of Perspex supported by chrome-effect poles glued at intervals. Set the shelves against a silver cardboard background to give the impression of a mirrored wall. This technique would also prove useful in other dollhouse scenes, such as a modern bathroom, a department store, or a stylish cocktail bar. Instructions are on page 114.

▲ CLOCK
A 1950s' clock set above the door is a lovely finishing touch for the diner scene. This clock has a hand-drawn face on cardboard framed by eight lengths of wooden molding with angled ends, glued together and sprayed with silver paint. A layout guide for this clock face is on page 117.

▶ JUKEBOX
A jukebox gives a perfect finishing touch to this scene—one of the reasons why the diner became such a popular place for teenagers to hang out and to listen to the exciting new rock 'n' roll music that swept America in the 1950s. This jukebox is a porcelain replica of a contemporary Wurlitzer. Create your own jukebox from a domed block of wood, with raised features created from half-round dowel painted silver, and panels colored with metallic paints.

▲ FOOD, GLASSES, AND PLATES
No diner would be complete without platefuls of food, menus, crockery, and glassware. Identical sets of plastic crockery, available from dollhouse suppliers, are ideal. Stacks of plates can also be created from white cardboard, to fill the shelves above and behind the bar to give an impression of a well-stocked diner.

▼ DOOR
Covered in wood-effect paper, and framed with wood strip colored with silver metallic paint, this door has been finished with a frosted panel cut from a plastic box. Diners were often advertised with a simple neon message such as "Eat Here" or a logo showing a similar theme. For this diner, a knife-and-fork logo was drawn on paper with a gray pen, then photocopied onto a plastic sheet and secured behind the frosted panel; the logo is on page 117

▲ VINYL SEATING
Families or groups of teenagers can enjoy sitting together across a diner table loaded with good things to eat. Created on an L-shaped wooden unit, the seating is made quite simply from leather-effect plasticized fabric quilted onto rectangles of soft blanket fabric. See page 116 for instructions.

ADD TO THE LOOK

▲ LIGHTING
Strips along the ceiling gave a practical light for diners, to complement the natural light from the large windows overlooking the dining tables. In addition, a strip of lights above the glass shelving made the stock of glass and chinaware an attractive feature, welcoming customers and promising a bountiful supply of food and drink. Lights set into the ceiling and above the glass shelves can be created with a frame of wooden molding sprayed silver, with a rectangle of thick tracing paper glued on top. This disperses the light and gives a softened effect.

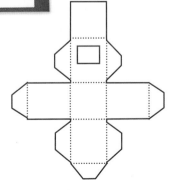

Use the template on the left to cut a classic paper napkin dispenser from silver cardboard. Score along the dotted lines on the reverse of the cardboard and cut out the small rectangle on the front face. Fold up the shape around a stack of tissue squares, and glue the cardboard tabs in place. Add silver beads as feet. Salt and pepper shakers can be made from tiny lengths of clear Perspex tube, filled with white or gray polymer clay, and capped with tiny buttons sprayed silver. Make a tomato sauce bottle from red polymer clay with a white clay top, and glue on a paper label.

BAR

This bar can be quickly and effectively constructed using ³/₁₆ in. (5mm) thick poly-board, which is available from art stores. Poly-board is thin Styrofoam sheeting sandwiched between smooth outer layers of cardboard. It can be cut with a sharp craft knife. When the bar is complete, add a napkin dispenser using the template.

❶ From poly-board, cut a counter. The size will depend on the size of your room. Use paper templates until you are happy with the proportions. Glue 3¹³/₁₆ in. (97mm) tall rectangles of poly-board at intervals around the curve and along the straight edge, about ⅝ in. (16mm) in from the edge. Hold them upright with cardboard positioned at right angles behind them.

❷ Cover the front of the bar with a strip of firm cardboard, curved into shape and glued in position against the poly-board uprights. Cover the surface with leather-effect plasticized fabric, or with tiles to match the floor.

❸ Glue textured paper to the top surface of the bar, leaving an extra ¾ in. (20mm) of paper around the edges. Around the curves, use scissors to cut tabs into the paper, up to the edge of the bar. Fold the paper under the edge and glue it in place.

❹ Cut a length of ¹/₁₆ in. (2mm) thick, ¼ in. (6mm) wide aluminum strip. Bend it into shape against the poly-board, and then glue it in place. Alternatively, use a ¼ in. (6mm) wide strip of silver cardboard.

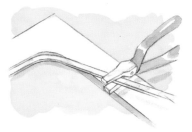

❺ Turn the bar upside down and draw round the top on scrap paper. For a foot rail, cut a length of ³/₁₆ in. (5mm) circular aluminum bar. Using pliers, bend the rail against the edge of a table until it is the shape of the drawn line. Bend it gradually, checking the bar against the drawing after each stage.

❻ Using ¼ in. (6mm) wide flexible metal strip or a ¼ in. (6mm) strip of thick silver cardboard, bend a holding bracket and glue it to the rail. Make a slit in the bar edge and poke the end of the bracket through. Secure behind the bar with epoxy glue.

GLASS SHELVES

Ideally, the glass shelves will be set into an alcove lit from above by a strip of lighting. This gives an attractive effect suited to a diner, public house, or cocktail bar.

❶ Line the wall with silver cardboard, glued in place. Cut lengths of ⅝ in. (16mm) wide, ¹/₁₆ in. (2mm) thick clear Perspex strip, to fit neatly inside the alcove. With a pencil and ruler, draw lines on the wall to mark the position of the shelves.

❷ Press pins into the wall along the marked line. Run a thin layer of white wood glue evenly along the back and side edges of the Perspex and stick it in position, with the pins holding it up. When thoroughly dry, remove the pins.

❸ Color ⅛ in. (3mm) diameter wooden dowel with silver metallic paint. Cut lengths to fit from the floor to the ceiling, then use epoxy glue to fix them at regular intervals to the shelves as supports.

BAR STOOL

The visual effect of the American diner is best achieved by choosing materials that epitomize the look of the period. Look out for silver-colored components or objects that can be sprayed silver to take their place in the diner as chrome fittings. Ribbed key rings, for example, give these bar stools their classic 1950s' appeal.

MAKING THE CUSHION

❶ Draw two circles, 1¼ in. (32mm) in diameter, on the back of thin leather-effect plasticized fabric. Cut out the circles, leaving a ⅜ in. (10mm) seam allowance. On another piece of fabric, draw two parallel lines 5⁄16 in. (8mm) apart and 4¼ in. (108mm) long. Cut out the strip, leaving a ⅜ in. (10mm) seam allowance on each long side.

❷ Using dark red thread and with the right sides of the fabric together, sew the strip to one of the circles, carefully matching up the drawn lines. Where the ends of the strip meet, sew them together in a straight line and trim off the excess fabric. Sew the second circle in place in the same way, completely closing the shape.

MAKING THE BASE

❶ Using hot glue or epoxy glue, stick two 1 in. (25mm) diameter key rings together and then to the base of the cushion. Leave under a weight to set.

❸ Using scissors, cut a cross shape in one of the circles, and use this hole to turn the piece right side out.

❹ Cut a 1¼ in. (32mm) diameter circle of cardboard and slip it into the cushion to lie flat underneath the top surface. Add foam or polyester stuffing, and then sew up the hole.

❷ Cut four lengths of 5⁄32 in. (4mm) diameter wooden dowel or aluminum rod, each 2¾ in. (70mm) long. If using dowel, color it with silver paint. Use epoxy glue to stick the ends inside the key rings, pushing the ends firmly against the cushion. Use a felt-tip pen to mark each leg ⅞ in (22mm) down from the key rings.

❸ With a file, roughen four patches at regular intervals on the inside of a 1¼ in. (32mm) diameter key ring. Attach the ring to the legs at the level of the felt-tip marks with epoxy glue. Before the glue sets, adjust the ring to ensure that the stool will stand correctly.

VINYL SEATING UNIT

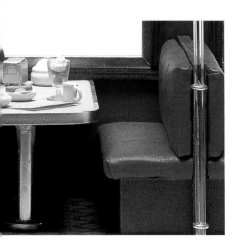

Comfortable padded seating was designed to maximize the space in the diner, with fixed seating units and tables secured to the floor and wall. The familiar metal-edged tables and pole legs would also be suitable for a fast-food restaurant or café.

The following instructions describe how to make a vinyl padded cushion. You will need to make one for each seat and one for each backrest.

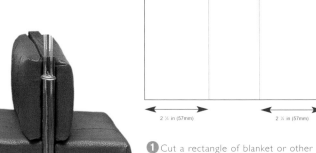

1 Cut a rectangle of blanket or other thick fabric, 1¾ x 5⅛ in. (45 x 130mm). From leather-effect plasticized fabric, cut a rectangle 3½ x 6¼ in. (90 x 158mm). Draw parallel lines on the back of the fabric, as shown in the layout.

2 ¼ in (57mm)   2 ¼ in (57mm)

WATER BOILER

Water boilers can be made from lengths of metal plumbing pipe. Glue circles of cardboard to the top and bottom, and smaller circles on the lid to give shaping. Add a small bead handle on top. The lower part of each tap is cut from a tiny curve of wood. Half of a dressmaker's pop fastener forms the tap handle. Spray the completed model with silver metallic enamel paint.

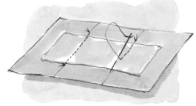

2 Sew the blanket to the plasticized fabric along the drawn lines, with a neat line of sewing in dark red thread.

5 Cut a rectangle of ³⁄₁₆ in. (5mm) thick Styrofoam board or thick cardboard, 3¼ x 5⅛ in. (82 x 130mm). Glue it upright, attached to the wall and floor in between two windows.

3 Cut a rectangle of ³⁄₁₆ in. (5mm) thick Styrofoam board or thick cardboard, 1¾ x 5⅛ in. (45 x 130mm). Glue it to the blanket fabric. Stick lengths of double-sided tape around the edge, and then fold the edges of the plasticized fabric over the edges and onto the tape.

6 Make two boxes from ³⁄₁₆ in. (5mm) Styrofoam board or thick cardboard, with the following measurements:
Ends: cut two pieces, each 1³⁄₁₆ x 1⅝ in. (30 x 41mm)
Front and back: cut two pieces, each 1³⁄₁₆ x 4¾ in. (30 x 120mm)
Assemble and glue them as shown in the diagram, cover with brown paper, then glue them in place on either side of the larger upright.

4 At the corners, fold the fabric into a triangle shape and tape flat. Make two cushions.

7 Glue the two padded cushions in place for each seat. Finish with two strips of ¼ in. (6mm) wide, ⅛ in. (3mm) thick wood, colored with mahogany stain and glued along the top and up the side of the seating unit.

DINING TABLE

Classic features of a diner table are a smooth chrome edging, curved corners, and chrome legs seated in disks set into the floor. Recreate this effect using modern materials such as aluminum strip, metal poles, and buttons painted silver. A mottled surface can be made from textured craft paper.

1 From ³⁄₁₆ in. (5mm) thick Styrofoam board, cut a rectangle 3¹⁄₁₆ × 4¹⁵⁄₁₆ in. (78 × 125mm). Position a coin on the corner of the table and draw round it. Use a craft knife to cut along the outer part of the line to make a curved table edge. Repeat on the other corner of the short side of the table.

2 Holding the same coin in a vise, bend a length of ¹⁄₁₆ in. (2mm) thick, ¼ in. (6mm) wide aluminum strip around it to match the curve on the foam board. Shape the aluminum strip to fit along three edges of the table.

3 Cover the tabletop in textured paper, and then glue the aluminum strip around the edge.

4 Cut two 2⅛ in. (54mm) lengths of ⅜ in. (10mm) diameter wooden dowel. Glue a wooden button to one end of each piece, then spray the legs and button base with silver metallic paint. Glue the legs to the floor, and then glue the table on top, with the straight edge glued to the wall.

FOOD, CROCKERY, AND GLASSES

1 Have fun creating a tasty menu for your American diner, being sure to include classic goodies such as eggs and sausages, waffles, pancakes, hamburgers, hotdogs, milk shakes, mugs of coffee, donuts, and, of course, cheesecake. This selection of food was created with polymer clay, which can be modeled into detailed shapes, then baked to form hard, permanent items.

2 Sets of white plastic crockery, available from dollhouse suppliers, are ideal to stock the diner. Create piles of plates to stack behind the bar from ⅞ in. (22mm) diameter circles of white cardboard, separated by ½ in. (12mm) diameter circles of thick white cardboard.

3 Cut lengths of ⁵⁄₁₆ in. (8mm) diameter Perspex tube as glass tumblers. Fill some with colored polymer clay, such as orange to resemble orange juice. A sliver of wood, colored with a felt-tip pen, can be inserted as a drinking straw.

4 Reduce the front page of a newspaper using a photocopier (you may need to repeat the reduction several times to make the page small enough), then fold it around some blank pages and leave under a heavy book to press flat.

OTHER DETAILS

To make a clock, copy the clock layout guide onto card and color the details with felt-tip pen. Frame with sectons of wooden molding. Glue them together in a frame, spray silver, then glue to the clock face.

Draw the diner logo onto tracing paper using a permanent marker. Turn the paper over, spray with glue then smooth onto the back of a glass door.

PERIOD POINTS

• Modern modeling materials can be used to capture the unmistakable chrome, mirror, and perspex elements of a 1950s' American diner.

• Coordinate the color scheme with leather-effect vinyl fabric, used for the stool cushions, bar surround, and diner walls.

• Bars of thin wooden doweling, glued to the wall in threes, can be sprayed with silver enamel paint to give a classic chrome finish.

• Have fun creating food and drink for the American diner from polymer clay—a cheesecake, burgers, french fries, hotdogs, and familiar details such as a bottle of tomato ketchup.

1960s
country kitchen

Roast chicken, fruit, and cheese for a Sunday lunch.

A country kitchen in the 1960s was a picture of functionality and simple design governed by ease of use and cleanliness. Modern understanding of hygiene—from the 1950s onwards—led to white becoming the standard color for kitchens and kitchen goods with just a few touches of color to add personality and warmth. The overall effect is of a light, fresh, crisp quality evoking sunny mornings and a busy housewife keeping control of all aspects of household life. Because the domestic kitchen is generally the preserve of women, the finishing touches to the kitchen design tend to be feminine: ruched drapes, jugs of flowers, and floral print fabrics for items such as oven gloves, and a cushion for the kitchen chair. The following chapter offers advice and designs to recreate some of the classic features of a 1960s kitchen using basic materials and simple techniques.

Pretty fabrics for a feminine touch.

THE BASICS

MAKING A FLOOR
Vinyl tiles made for a full-size house are a good source of flooring for a modern dollhouse kitchen. Choose a tile design that will not dominate the room. Use either muted colors or a small repeat design that mimics tiny tiles. Remove fittings and furniture from the room and cut a single vinyl piece to cover the whole floor. Glue it in place.

◄TILES
Dollhouse tiles are available in many designs in both square and border tiles. They are incorporated into the kitchen design to surround the counters, as they are easy to keep clean and offer an opportunity for a splash of color and floral or geometric designs. An alternative is to cover the area with tile-effect paper.

◄THE WALLS
Most of the walls are plastered plain white. Some areas, such as a wall between the kitchen and a stairwell or store cupboard, can be covered with strips of pine to give the impression of tongue-and-groove paneling. These can also be painted white and finished with matte varnish.

FURNITURE AND FITTINGS

▶ CHAIR

A kitchen chair is hardwearing and practical, finished in hard gloss varnish to survive the knocks and spillages of a busy kitchen. Made in pinewood, it fits with almost any style or color scheme used in a modern kitchen. The addition of a soft cushion tied on to the seat with leg ribbons will link the chair in with the décor. Instructions for making this cushion are on page 122.

▲ GLASS-FRONTED CABINET

In a functional room useful items are visible to the eye so that they can be used regularly with ease, and anyone can find them. Glass-fronted cabinets are ideal for this: the busy housewife can see at a glance what needs to be purchased and what is running out—essential for keeping the household running. See page 122.

▼ REFRIGERATOR

No modern kitchen would be complete without a refrigerator bursting with food. Instructions on page 123 show how to make a basic white fridge. All styles of fridges are available commercially.

SALAD BOWLS

During the 1960s, fresh salad items became available all year round, and with new knowledge of the health-giving properties of fresh fruit and vegetables, a big wooden salad-serving bowl became an essential piece of kitchen equipment. Salad bowls and their contents can be created with polymer clay. See page 124.

▼ WINDOW

A lovely casement window can be opened in the summer to let light and air into the room. This window has been embellished with gingham drapes created from patterned fabric or ribbon. It is also the ideal place to display a bowl full of flowers to brighten up the kitchen. Instructions for both these items are on page 125.

▼ WASH DAY

With the days of servants long gone, machines started to take the place of staff after the 1950s, relieving householders of the grind of daily chores. A washing machine is an essential item for this kitchen, accompanied by a clotheshorse and a washing line.

▶ COOKER

A clean-cut electric cooker is the central item around which the other items in the kitchen are grouped. It should be positioned next to a counter where baking trays can be placed ready to put into the oven and where hot items can be left to cool. A cooker hood completes the set-up, designed to remove the smells and steam from the cooking area making it a more pleasant place in which to work.

▼ BAKING DAY

One of the most evocative activities in any kitchen is baking day, when the smell of fresh bread spreads throughout the house, bringing a sense of warmth and comfort. A tray full of fresh loaves gives the impression of a contented household that enjoys its food.

ADD TO THE LOOK

LIGHTING

Electric overhead lighting is appropriate for a modern kitchen scene. A lampshade can be created out of a small plastic dollhouse bowl or half a plastic egg. Trim the opening into a decorative crown shape. Drill a hole in the end large enough to fit the bulb and fitting, and with a little extra room to avoid burning the lampshade. Glue decorative gold braid and a beaded strip around the edge of the shade, and then glue in place on the ceiling.

Jam pots with gingham fabric-covered lids can be made from lengths of perspex tube filled with red polymer clay. Glue the fabric on top and tie with a strand of embroidery floss. Jars can be made from polymer clay. Add labels cut from colored paper, and lids from circles cut from cork mat.

CHAIR CUSHION

A kitchen chair can be made more comfortable to allow a dollhouse cook, exhausted after a long day preparing food, to sit and enjoy a quiet moment reading the newspaper or having a cup of coffee. An attractive cushion can be added to the chair and tied in place with colored ribbons.

1 Cut two squares of patterned cotton fabric, ¾ in. (20mm) bigger than the square of the chair seat, and one square of thin foam the same size as the chair seat.

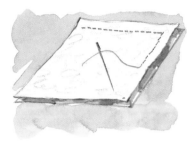

2 With right sides together, sew the two pieces of fabric together along three edges, leaving a ⅜ in. (10mm) seam. Trim across the corners.

4 With tiny stitches, attach four lengths of ribbon to the corners of the cushion and tie them around the chair legs.

3 Turn right side out and fill with the foam. Tuck in the raw edges of the fabric and sew the opening to close it.

A PAINTED CHAIR

Sand a ready-made pine chair thoroughly, to remove the varnish and to give a slightly rough surface on which the paint can adhere. Paint the chair with acrylic paint—white, pastel blue, or pink will look particularly effective. For a stencil pattern, add a simple floral design on the back bar. Finish with acrylic varnish.

GLASS-FRONTED CABINET

A glass-fronted cabinet is an attractive addition to a wall, displaying interesting contents such as colorful crockery, groceries, or storage jars. A plain-fronted cabinet can be given a glass front, or a small box or trunk can be converted into a cabinet.

1 Remove the hinges and doors from an existing cabinet, or remove the lid from a wooden box or trunk.

2 Glue two tiny strips of wood to the inside of the cabinet as shelf supports, then cut a rectangle of ⅛ in. (3mm) thick wood as a shelf, and glue in position.

3 For a two-door cabinet: from ⅛ in. (3mm) thick wood, cut four ⁵⁄₁₆ in. (8mm) wide strips that are half the width of the aperture in the front of the cabinet. Cut four strips that are the height of the aperture minus ⅝ in. (16mm). Assemble and glue the pieces together to form two frames as shown.

4 Cut rectangles of thin Perspex slightly bigger than the inside line of the doorframes and draw round them on to the back of the wood. Use a craft knife to trim away a shallow layer of wood to receive the Perspex. Sand and paint the frames, then glue the Perspex in place.

5 Attach the doors with tiny brass hinges and add handles (both available from specialist dollhouse suppliers). Alternatively, handles can be created by gluing colored or brass beads in position.

REFRIGERATOR

Invented in 1913, the refrigerator quickly became an essential piece of kitchen equipment. It allowed foods to be kept for longer and ended the reliance on the iceman or an ice-cream seller in the hot summer months. A modern well-stocked refrigerator is the place that every member of the family visits at some point during the day, whether to fetch a chilled beer or to snack on the remains of yesterday's meal. A dollhouse refrigerator can be bought commercially, or can be created by painting a dollhouse chest white, or white and dark blue, and standing it on end.

STOCKING UP

The shelves and drawers of a refrigerator should be stocked with good things to eat. The plastic door shelves on the left are created from the protective plastic covers from disposable razors. They can be filled with fruit and vegetables created from colored polymer clay. Create textures on the sides of the vegetables with a knife or skewer. Add leaves from dried foliage or grass, and stalks from tiny strips of wood. Food can also be stacked onto plates or into containers to stack inside.

❶ Take a bought dollhouse chest and stand it on its end. Shelves can be added to the inside. Glue strips of wood or short thin sticks to the inside walls to act as shelf supports. Glue strips of wood to the bottom to act as feet. When dry, paint white. Cut a rectangle of thin Perspex as a "glass" shelf to sit on top.

❷ The protective plastic covers from disposable razors make ideal door shelves for the inside of a refrigerator. Use contact adhesive or hot glue to attach two or three to the inside of the door, and then fill with tiny bottles, vegetables, and food packets.

❸ For an icebox, add a door to a small box by gluing a strip of fabric hinge first to a rectangle of plastic cut from packaging (such as a hard plastic wallet file or a plastic fruit box) and then to the top of the box. Glue the unit inside the top of the refrigerator.

❹ For a handle, cut a 1 in. (25mm) length of ⅛ in. (3mm) square wood strip and color it with silver metallic enamel paint. Glue in place on the front of the refrigerator.

SALAD BOWLS

1 Prepare some polymer clay by rubbing it and rolling it between your hands until pliable. Select a mold around which to form the clay. This might be a domed metal lid from a bathroom product or the end of a tool handle, such as an awl. The item must be able to withstand low heat.

2 Mold the clay around the end of the lid or handle, pressing it into shape evenly. Take care not to make a bowl whose walls curve inwards; otherwise it will not be possible to remove the mold.

3 Trim the top of the clay with a craft knife to form the rim of the bowl.

4 Form a small circle of clay and attach it to the base of the bowl, smoothing the edges into the main shape.

5 Bake the whole piece with the mold in place, following the manufacturer's instructions. When baked and cool to the touch, twist the bowl until it releases from the mold.

6 Press out tiny, irregular pieces of green polymer clay and tiny spheres of red polymer clay on to a piece of cardboard. Bake to harden, and then pile into the bowls as salad.

BREAD TRAY

1 From ⅛ in. (3mm) wood, cut the following:
Front and back: two pieces, each ⅜ × 1½ in. (10 × 38mm)
Sides: two pieces, each ⅜ × 2 in. (10 × 50mm)
Base: one piece, 1½ in. × 2¼ in. (38 × 58mm)

2 In each of the front and back pieces, use a ⅛ in. (3mm) drill bit to make two holes defining the ends of the hand holes. Use a craft knife to carve out the wood in-between. Finish with fine-grit paper or a mouse-tail rasp.

3 Assemble and glue the pieces together as shown in the diagram. Sand the tray, then finish with varnish.

VEGETABLE RACK

The bread tray pattern can also be used to make a wooden vegetable rack—a useful addition to a modern kitchen. This can be fitted into an existing kitchen unit. Remove the door and shelves from a bought kitchen cupboard. Make three trays following the instructions, making the tray as wide and long as the inside of your cupboard. Glue strips of 1/8 in (3mm) square wood as drawer runners on the walls of the cupboard. Fill the trays with fruit and vegetables.

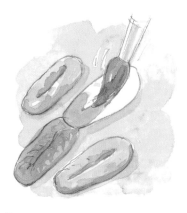

4 Model loaves of bread out of pale brown polymer clay. Once the models are baked and hard, add the effect of baking by stippling the top surface of the bread with ochre acrylic paint, add a little warm brown and stipple again. Finally, add a little black to the paint mix and stipple the topmost surfaces.

CURTAINS

The following instructions are for a window with a window ledge. If your dollhouse has no window ledges and you would like your curtains to be longer, follow the same instructions but use longer pieces of fabric.

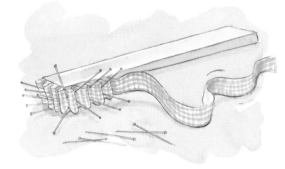

1 Cut two pieces of gingham fabric or ribbon, each the height of your window and about three-quarters of the width of the whole window. If using fabric, add a ¾ in. (20mm) seam allowance to each measurement. Roll and sew a small hem around all sides. If using ribbon, hem along the bottom edge only.

2 Sew a line of running stitch along the top of one curtain and gather it up until it is the width of half the window. Secure the thread with a few stitches and repeat for the other curtain. Glue the curtains to the top of the window.

3 To make a valance board, use ⅛ in. (3mm) thick wood and cut a ½ in. (12mm) wide strip ½ in. (12mm) longer than the width of the whole window.

4 Glue a length of ⅜ in. (10mm) ribbon to three edges of the valance board, pinning it into folds along the way. Leave the pins in position while the glue dries, and then remove. Glue the board into position, like a shelf above the window, and butting up to the frame.

5 Tie back the curtains with embroidery floss or more ribbon.

A BOWL OF FLOWERS

• These yellow buds are made from artificial stamens sold for use by flower arrangers. They have waxy threads that can be curved and will hold the shape well when displayed in a bowl. Fill the bowl with modeling clay, then push the ends of the stamens into the clay.

• The plant leaves are made from strips of green paper trimmed into pointed leaf shapes. Curve each leaf by running it between your fingernails. Fix each leaf into the bowl with a dab of white glue.

PERIOD POINTS

• The projects in this chapter can be adapted
to fit other modern kitchen styles. For a
contemporary look, choose chrome fittings such
as handles and bars, and paint the kitchen units
in a striking color, finished with acrylic varnish.

• A few carefully selected ornaments will add
character to the kitchen. Paint a button with the
face of a sun to appear above the door, and place
tiny pots and tins on the tops of the cupboards,
decorated with painted flowers.

• Tinware pitchers, bowls, and buckets are an
attractive addition to this kitchen scene. To unify
the look, paint the pieces with white enamel paint.
Add a fine line of dark blue paint around the rims
and on the handles.

• Stock the cupboards and refrigerator with
plenty of miniature food. Tins can be made
from lengths of dowel painted silver and wrapped
with tiny paper labels. Boxes and cartons can
be made from folded card, filled with food made
from polymer clay.

Create a stylish CD rack from black cardboard with tiny colorful cardboard CDs.

Modern apartment

An interesting theme in modern living is the conversion of decommissioned industrial buildings into fashionable apartment blocks. These apartments are characterized by high ceilings and strong architectural features, such as brick pillars, open stairways, brick-arched windows, steel girders, and frosted glass features—as used in the gallery that frames this stylish sitting room. The structure of the room demonstrates how a large warehouse can be transformed into a domestic setting without losing the connection with its industrial heritage. Tall warehouse windows with classic industrial tracery are celebrated as a main feature in this apartment conversion. An added gallery floor divides the windows in half but leaves the complete shapes visible, allowing light to flood into the room. The frosted glass on the gallery picks up the windows' geometric pattern to underpin a unified design theme that is echoed in the square coffee table, the bold colored cushions, and the pattern of the girders. In this chapter, you can learn how to create some of the essential features of a modern apartment setting, from an open stairway to a CD rack and laptop computer.

Display a collection of beautiful beads and pebbles in a stainless-steel bowl.

THE BASICS

◀ MAKING A FLOOR

A large rug can be made from linen fabric. Remove a few threads from each side to give fringed edges. Hardwearing natural fibers such as rattan are popular textured floor coverings in modern city apartments. This effect can be achieved using handmade paper, available from craft and art stores. The paper used in this scene is made from banana leaves and other exotic plant fibers. Cut pieces to fit the room and secure to the floor with white glue.

◀ BRICK PILLARS

In apartment blocks created from converted warehouses and factories, high ceilings and impressive arched windows make attractive features to complement the clean-cut designs of modern furniture. In this scene, brick pillars reveal the origins of this industrial building. Cover the pillars first in cream-colored paper and then add brick shapes cut from watercolor paper stippled with brick-colored acrylic paints.

▲ GIRDERS

Industrial materials—brickwork and steel girders—feature in this room. These miniature girders have a fretwork section cut from thick cardboard, using the guide below. Glue this piece upright between two ⅛ in. (3mm) thick pieces of ¼ in. (6mm) wide wood strip. Paint blue, then varnish. Glue the girder strips under the gallery floor, between the pillars.

girder cutting guide

FURNITURE AND FITTINGS

▲ SOFA AND CHAIR
This sofa and chair are based on a clean-cut Scandinavian design. Two uprights and two long sections of light-colored pine board support padded cushions creating comfortable and versatile seating. Patterns and instructions for this furniture are given on page 130.

◀ SIDE TABLE
The legs of this side table are created from lengths of aluminum strip—available from model shops—bent into shape, and then glued to the base of a rectangle of ⅛ in. (3mm) thick wood. To protect the floor, sand the ends of the aluminum strip and cover each foot with black paper.

▲ CD RACK AND STEREO
A large warehouse room is the perfect acoustic space for playing music from this powerful system. Place the stereo on a side table and the second speaker at a strategic point in the room where the occupant might best enjoy the stereo effect. The stereo and speakers are made from pictures cut from an electrical catalog mounted onto small cardboard boxes.

▼ COFFEE TABLE
A large square of wooden board, supported on short, square-cut legs and mounted on domed bead feet, is one of the simplest pieces of furniture to create. Choose a piece of board with a fine grain to give an attractive surface when sanded and varnished. A highly polished surface is the perfect setting for a few carefully selected items, such as a vase of flowers and a large stainless-steel bowl filled with stones and glass balls.

▶ LIGHTING
Echoing the arches of the warehouse windows, this freestanding lamp is based on a classic Arco model by the designer Castiglioni. An elegant arc of brushed aluminum set into a block of marble provides an intense direct light for reading.

◀ LAPTOP
An essential item of urban living, a black laptop is an unmistakable hallmark of a modern city apartment. This tiny computer was created from two thick pieces of board, hinged with paper and covered with the detailed keyboard and screen pattern provided on page 131.

▶ FROSTED GLASS GALLERY
To ensure that the living room benefits from light from the tall warehouse windows, frosted glass panels form the walls of the upper gallery. In this dollhouse scene, the panels are made from strips of Perspex, with frosting created from tracing paper. Follow the instructions on page 133 to create your own frosted glass gallery.

◀ DISPLAY SHELVES
Mimicking the zigzag shape of the edge of the stairs, these stepped shelves provide space to display three attractive pots. Cut six rectangles of ⅛ in. (3mm) thick wood and glue them together in a zigzag shape. Varnish to finish, and then use impact adhesive to attach the shelves to the wall.

ADD TO THE LOOK

STAIRWAY
The shape of this warehouse space has been exploited to the full, using the whole height of the main room. Around the edges of the living room, a gallery has been installed to give access to bedrooms and a bathroom on an added upper floor. A stairway to join the two can be created quite simply from two matching zigzag stepped pieces cut from foam board. Detailed instructions are on page 133.

Plants and flowers soften the effect of the otherwise stark design of a modern interior. Carefully selected irises echo the blue of the furnishings downstairs, bringing a touch of color to the upper gallery. On the brick pillars, you can install plant containers to display trailing ivy and large ox-eye daisies. The instructions on page 132 show you how to re-create these floral arrangements.

SOFA AND CHAIR

Scandinavian designs for chairs are popular for modern interiors because of their stylish simplicity. Many are transported as flat kits, to be assembled in situ. The upholstery provides bold blocks of color within the room, against which colorful cushions can be displayed. This sofa and chair have been covered in the same material as the floor covering, to coordinate the décor. Choose touches of blue in the girders and iris flowers to echo this color scheme.

chair and sofa
support template

❶ For the sofa, from ³⁄₁₆ in. (5mm) thick wood, cut one seat section, 2½ x 6½ in. (65 x 165mm) and one back section, 1⅜ x 6½ in. (35 x 165mm). Copy the support template onto paper and draw round it twice on ³⁄₁₆ in. (5mm) thick wood, and use a jig saw to cut the pieces out. Sand all of the pieces.

❷ Glue the pieces together as shown in the diagram. Varnish to finish.

❸ For the padded cushions for the sofa, cut two pieces of fabric, each 7½ in. (190mm) (top edge) by 5¾ in. (145mm), and two pieces of ¼ in. (6mm) thick foam sheet, each 2¾ x 6½ in. (70 x 165mm). Fold each piece of fabric in half, so that the top edges meet. Sew the two short ends together, leaving a ½ in. (12mm) seam allowance. Turn right side out and fill with the foam.

❹ Tuck the raw edges of the fabric inside and sew the edge shut. Make the second padded cushion in the same way. Sew the two padded cushions together, and then glue them to the wooden seat.

CHOOSING A FABRIC

A plain hard-wearing coarse-weave fabric has been used in this room for both the upholstery and the large rug, giving the room a unified color scheme. Corduroy velvet would also be suitable, and woven fabrics with a subtle repeat pattern across the surface. To adapt this furniture for a 1960s sitting room, you could use brashly colored cotton print fabric.

SCATTER CUSHIONS

Bold blocks of color can be added to the room in the form of simple scatter cushions. Cut two 2 in. (50mm) squares of felt and sew them together around three edges. Stuff then sew the final edge together, making sure not to trap any of the stuffing in the seam. When finished, roll the cushion between your hands to encourage the stuffing to spread evenly around the cushion.

CHAIR

For the chair, follow the instructions for the sofa, using the following measurements:
From ³⁄₁₆ in. (5mm) thick wood, cut one seat section, 2½ x 3¼ in. (65 x 83mm) and one back section, 1⅜ x 3¼ in. (35 x 83mm).

For the padded cushions for the chair, cut two pieces of fabric, each 4¼ in. (108mm) (top edge) by 5¾ in. (145mm), and two pieces of ¼ in. (6mm) thick foam sheet, each 2¾ x 3¼ in. (70 x 83mm).

COFFEE TABLE

A low coffee table is a useful setting on which to display that iconic accessory of modern city living— a laptop computer. It is also a good space for a large bowl full of colored stones and glass to bring a splash of color and cool beauty to the otherwise austerely furnished room. This table is created simply from a large square of board mounted onto wooden legs, with metal feet created from small domed buttons.

1 From ¾ in. (5mm) thick wood, cut a 3¹⁵⁄₁₆ in. (100mm) square. Sand thoroughly, stain, and varnish.

2 From ½ in. (12mm) square wood strip, cut four legs, each ¾ in. (20mm) long. Use a sharp knife to trim off the bottom corners, to give four triangular faces as shown. Sand, stain, and varnish.

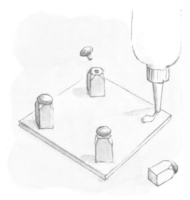

3 Cut a small notch in the base of each leg large enough to hold the shank of a small domed metallic button.

4 Glue a domed button to the bottom of each leg, then glue the legs to the underside of the table.

ELECTRICAL EQUIPMENT

No modern apartment would be complete without a range of electrical equipment, created here with scraps of cardboard and paper.

laptop template

MUSIC SYSTEM
This stereo and speakers are based on small cardboard boxes. Cut pictures of stereo equipment from an electrical catalog to cover the boxes. The boxes for the speakers were covered in colored paper, and then finished with an image of the speaker cone and controls, again cut from an electrical catalog.

LAPTOP
Cut three rectangles of ¹⁄₁₆ in. (2mm) thick cardboard, each ⅞ x 1¼ in. (22 x 32mm). Glue two together for the base. Photocopy the cover template onto paper and glue it around the cardboard pieces to make the base and lid. Use a permanent felt-tip pen to touch up any white edges that show. Fold the lid over to meet the keyboard.

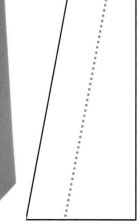

POWER SOCKET
Cut a tiny rectangle of thick cardboard. Use a black felt-tip pen to mark it with sockets, and then glue it to the skirting board. Glue a tiny scrap of wood to one socket and paint it black. Attach a thread cable to the wood, and the other end to the back of the stereo.

CD RACK
Cut two side pieces from black cardboard, using the template. Cut a rectangle of black cardboard, 3⅞ x ½ in. (99 x 12mm) and glue it between the side pieces in the position marked by a dotted line. Glue about 26 shelves between the uprights, each ½ x ⅜ in. (12 x 10 mm). Make CDs from cardboard, ⁷⁄₁₆ in. (11mm) square.

CD rack template

FLOWERS AND PLANTS

The striking lines of this warehouse room can be softened by the addition of a few strategically positioned floral arrangements. Containers of plants divide the pillars into visually pleasing sections, and vases of blue irises look beautiful displayed on the gallery and coffee table; set against a plain white background, they look particularly striking. Create these flowers and plants from scraps of colored paper.

VASE OF IRISES

iris template

1 Copy the iris template onto paper and cut it out. Draw round it on blue tissue paper and cut it out. Roll the tissue around the point of a wooden skewer and glue it into a cone. Remove the skewer. Prepare three for each flower stem.

FLOWER CONTAINERS

1 Cut a large plastic dollhouse bowl in half. Sand the outsides of the pieces to roughen the surface, and then paint with acrylic paint. Varnish to finish. Glue the bowl pieces to the pillars.

2 Cut lengths of thin wire and curve them to hook over the edge of the bowl. Glue the end in place inside the bowl, using impact adhesive. Paint the wire green with a little white glue mixed in.

2 Mix yellow paint with a little white glue, and then use it to paint the end of a piece of thin wire.

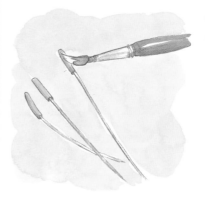

3 Push wire into the center of each blue cone. Pull through until only the yellow tip shows. Secure with white glue. Prepare three for each flower stem.

3 Cut tiny ivy leaves from cream paper. Use a felt-tip pen to make green marks on the leaves. Glue them at intervals along the hanging wires.

4 Fill the plant containers with green sponge or flower-arranger's foam. Cut a circle of white paper for a large daisy, and trim the edge into a fringe. Push a yellow glass-headed quilter's pin through the center and into the sponge.

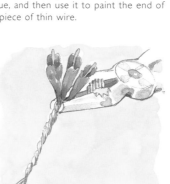

4 Hold three cones at their bases in pliers. Twist the loose ends of wire together. Paint the wire green with acrylic paint mixed with white glue.

5 With white glue, secure long leaf shapes cut from thin green cardboard in a small vase. Add two or three irises, and bend the flowers into natural positions.

FROSTED GLASS GALLERY

This technique of imitating frosted glass is very useful in a variety of dollhouse settings. Simple patterns—such as this geometric design—suit a modern apartment. It could also be used for shower doors in a stylish bathroom. The logo of a company could be cut into the design for use in an office, or you could make detailed panels for a store window. In each case, the design can be cut from good-quality, thick tracing paper (sometimes sold as "layout paper") and attached to the back of Perspex or glass panels with spray glue.

❶ Cut a panel of clear Perspex sheet to fit neatly between two pillars—either the brick-effect pillars or square wooden pillars fixed to the gallery.

❷ With a pencil, lightly draw out the design on to the tracing paper. It is a good idea to wash your hands first, as tracing paper can be very absorbent.

❸ Use a craft knife to cut out sections of the design. Spray the front of the tracing paper with spray mounting glue, and then smooth it onto the back of the Perspex.

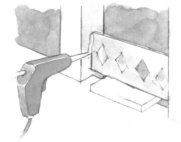

❹ Use hot glue or impact adhesive to secure the finished panel between the pillars. Rest the panel on a ⅜ in. (10mm) block while the glue dries, to hold it a little way above the floor.

❺ Glue a length of wood along the top of the Perspex to make a hand rail. Glue tiny strips of wood at the ends of the Perspex to disguise the joins between it and the pillars.

STAIRS

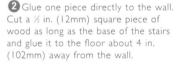

An open stairway is a striking addition to a modern apartment scene, providing architectural interest and a sense of height. Plain plaster walls and wooden treads are a classic design and can be added to almost any dollhouse setting. These stairs have been finished at the base with a skirting board cut from a strip of cream cardboard, to contrast slightly with the plain white wall.

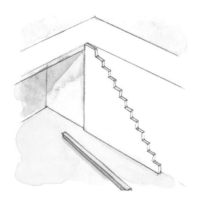

❶ Cut two stepped shapes from white foam board, reaching to the height of the gallery. Each rise and each tread should be about ⁹⁄₁₆ in. (15mm).

❷ Glue one piece directly to the wall. Cut a ½ in. (12mm) square piece of wood as long as the base of the stairs and glue it to the floor about 4 in. (102mm) away from the wall.

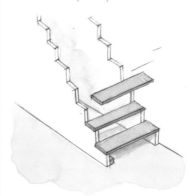

❸ Glue the second stepped piece to the wooden strut. Cut treads from ⅛ in. (3mm) thick wood, each long enough to fit neatly across the gap, and wide enough to fit neatly on the steps. Varnish each tread before gluing it in position.

ADDING A HAND RAIL

These stairs are designed to be quite plain and open. If you prefer to add a hand rail, fit two newel posts—one at the bottom and one at the top of the stairs. Each newel post could be made from a square wooden post with a bead ball on top. Fit a wooden hand rail between the posts. To complete the look, add a panel of frosted glass made following the instructions, left, using a sheared rectangle shape to run up the sides of the stairs.

doll gallery

Dolls and their costumes are just as much a part of dollhouse style as the furniture and accessories that have been explored in this book. Your choice of a doll family to inhabit your house is a crucial aspect of the whole design. Clothing fabrics and accessories are all subjects in which to immerse yourself. Whether you buy ready-dressed dolls or make costumes yourself, dolls in historical costume will bring your dollhouse to life.

This attractive Shaker woman would complete the Shaker scene on pages 56–63.

16TH-CENTURY TUDOR DOLLS

This Tudor family, with their fine clothing, would be the perfect inhabitants for the Tudor Banqueting Hall on pages 16–23.

Rich fabrics embellished with symbolic patterns worked in gold embroidery are characteristic features of this gentleman's fine attire. Shield designs, or representations of family emblems such as roses or lions, were popular embroidery motifs. His long coat, here made resplendent with a fur edging, has slashed sleeves that allow extra freedom of movement, but also reveal splashes of color to add to the look. The rich red also chimes with his splendid red velvet hat. A practical frocked garment underneath has square or "boxed" pleats, parted at the front to show woolen breeches and black woolen stockings.

By the age of just five or six, a little girl of the Tudor period would already be an accomplished seamstress and would be beginning to master the complicated art of running an efficient household. She would be assigned certain duties around the house, such as waiting upon her mother or helping her to make arrangements for formal banquets. This little girl's pretty flame-colored overdress is made from a rich satin fabric decorated only with a simple textured trim. Her hair is tied back and her under-dress has a high neckline, showing the importance of formality and modesty for young girls of the period.

Middle-class Tudor women were often managers of the household, sharing with their menfolk the hard work of keeping a house, with its many servants, cooks, and other staff, running smoothly and efficiently. Fashion of the time emphasized the stately qualities of the lady's demeanor—a tight waistline and a gold-trimmed neckline lent themselves to an elegant posture and an authoritative attitude to those around her. Jewelry included fine gold necklaces set with polished gemstones, and skillfully crafted baubles that could hang on the lady's waistband. For this elegant lady, great fur sleeves added to her impressive attitude, lending dignity and poise to the overall effect.

17TH-CENTURY STUART DOLLS

A 17th-century family resplendent in their lace-embellished costume.

This fine gentleman displays many of the hallmarks of clothing style in the 17th century. Sturdy breeches were tied at the waist with a fabric binding or a buttoned waistband. These ballooned out over the top of high leather boots suitable for horse-riding, sometimes topped with a wide band of lace. Lace also featured as a broad collar upon which loose curls of hair could drape. The gentleman's hat is a characteristic period touch. Pinned up at one side traditionally to allow him to carry a pike or standard into battle, this became an elegant fashion statement, completed by the addition of a fine feather.

For everyday wear, a young 17th-century boy might wear woolen breeches and a simple linen shirt to allow him the freedom to help out with his father's work, or to fight and tumble with his friends. Such items could withstand the wear-and-tear of a young boy's playful activities. For formal occasions, he would be expected to change into clothes such as those pictured here—a set of satin breeches and tunic, buttoned carefully at the front, and restricting the child to good behavior. Long hair was a distinctive look for little boys and grown men, falling onto a broad white collar—here edged with lace.

Women's fashion of the 17th century combined a flattering shape and decorative lace with practical fabrics that were both attractive and hard-wearing. A chemise— a simple shift-like dress— was the basic garment worn underneath the outer layers. This could be washed or replaced regularly, while outer clothing made in more expensive fabrics could last for many weeks or months without needing to be changed. This dress, in a rich orange hue, has just a touch of embroidered edging. The principle decorative effect comes from a large lace collar—sometimes home-crafted, but often imported from fine lace-makers in Holland or Italy.

18TH-CENTURY GEORGIAN DOLLS

For an 18th-century gentleman, good manners were everything, and clothing was designed around principles of polite social relationships. Young men were encouraged to learn how to sit and stand beautifully, showing off their shapely legs in smooth-fitting knitted stockings, and greeting both ladies and gentlemen with a gracious bow. Books were published comparing the relative merits of different hand gestures and postures to show off a man's social prowess. This gentleman's clothing is decorated with embroidery on his long coat and frocked vest. Flamboyant lace cuffs helped emphasize his conversation with well-practiced and courteous hand gestures.

This little girl's silk-satin dress and lace-fringed apron show that she is destined for a life of elegant dances and social interaction. Her education would have included training in polite topics of conversation, learning how to speak with respect to those higher up the social ladder, and mastering the steps of stately dances. These dances were known by all the young women of the day who hoped to meet their future husbands at formal social occasions. At more intimate social events, this little girl might also have been asked to show off her skills as a musician, playing a pretty tune on the harpsichord.

Formal occasions such as elegant receptions or dances were an important part of 18th-century social life for the wealthy classes. This lady's voluminous dress is constructed in a characteristic two-part style. For formal wear, over-dresses were made from luxurious fabrics such as silk velvet with a rich, attractive sheen. Above the waist, they were laced in a flattering pattern across the chest. The lower dress was held in shape by hoops set on an internal frame. These garments have been embellished by pretty embroidery with floral motifs. On dolls' clothing these can be hand-embroidered or cut from pieces of machine lace and sewn in position.

In their richly embroidered garments, this 18th-century family is well-prepared for a formal social occasion.

18TH-CENTURY REGENCY DOLLS

Like his prospective partner, this gentleman's clothing has a high waistline, flatteringly cut to emphasize his elegant posture. A band of patterned fabric, sometimes called a cummerbund, holds his trousers and shirt neatly in place at the waist. His jacket is cut just high enough to reveal the cummerbund, falling in elegant curves to either side in a tailed coat that is characteristic of the period. A formal collar and tightly fitting sleeves are softened by the addition of a touch of lace at the shirt collar. Tight-fitting long breeches and high riding boots topped with a gold border complete the look.

Anyone familiar with Jane Austen's novels will recognize the relationship between this little group of 18th-century figures. The only way a young woman could hope to climb the social ladder and ensure a secure future for her family was to make a suitable marriage, so social status and inherited wealth were critical factors in her marriage choice. For this reason, suitors were inspected and vetted by the young woman's mother or aunt, and meetings would take place under their watchful eyes. An extended period of courtship would allow all parties to come to the decision about whether this was an appropriate match.

Only if she had independent means, such as a fortune inherited from her husband or family, could an older woman expect to live in comfortable style in her own house. Otherwise, she had to rely upon the patronage of her daughter's husband—so it was in her own interest to ensure that her daughter married a man who combined physical prowess with a secure financial future. This lady's dress, in black with a small repeat pattern of floral sprigs, suggests that she may have been a widow for some years. Since women married very young, often to older men, this was a common situation.

A young woman is admired by her Regency suitor, under the watchful eye of her mother.

19TH-CENTURY VICTORIAN DOLLS

The master of the household, this statuesque gentleman was probably a a factory-owner, helping to oversee the new industrialized processes that led to an upsurge in manufacturered domestic products during the 19th century. His great fortune would be invested carefully in stocks and shares, building a secure future for his family. This careful and controlled approach to work was reflected in clothing of the period. Decoration for a gentleman was allowed only in a few tiny touches of luxury, such as a gold tie-pin. Extravagance was reserved for the women of the household. Otherwise, this gentleman's clothing was tightly buttoned in—just like his emotions.

This Victorian family, in their formal attire, would be likely to inhabit a town house such as the one on pages 80–87.

Depending on the social status of the family, this little girl might have been educated at home by a governess or sent to a private school which, during the 19th century, had started to accept girls. Along with reading, writing, and math, she would also learn the domestic arts such as embroidery and cookery. Her very first projects might be to make a dress, or to plan a meal. This little girl's comfortable clothing shows that while she would be expected to work diligently, she also had some freedom to play between classes, enjoying the skipping rhymes and songs popular in this period.

In everday life, a Victorian woman would have a range of comfortable yet formal dresses to choose from, plainly cut and shaped from attractive cotton-print fabrics. However, young women would also have a few special dresses for social occasions, such as this extravagantly layered and lace-edged gown in contrasting blue silk satins. Such dresses might be worn to events such as horse-racing or the opera— important gathering places for the wealthy middle classes. A matching satin parasol completes the look—an accessory that could be used for flirtation, but also to ensure that the lady maintained her fashionably pale skin.

20TH-CENTURY EDWARDIAN DOLLS

Joining his wife for their Sunday stroll, this Edwardian gentleman has a frocked coat, vest, and carefully creased trousers that are characteristic of the period. Many middle-class families turned out on a Sunday for their regular promenade—it was a chance to meet neighbors, to spend time witn the family, and to share quiet time together. Children were expected to be on their best behavior, and the whole family would dress in their best clothes to keep up good appearances. This gentleman's Sunday attire included a white satin tie, a top hat, and a small white flower in his buttonhole.

An Edwardian family in formal attire waits for their carriage to take them to visit friends.

A young girl of the Edwardian era enjoyed more freedoms than many of her historical counterparts, but it was not until the First World War that the majority of women were called upon to take part in regular working life and to contribute much more to society than polite conversation, bringing up the family, and running the household. By the Edwardian period, most girls received some education and might expect to have a paid job outside the household for some years of her life, but she would still be expected to give this up if she married.

Dignified clothing in royal purple, with an elegant train trailing behind, gives this Edwardian lady her impressive stature, showing that she is the true head of the household. Heavy satin fabrics, worked in many layers and panels, meant that an Edwardian lady's formal attire weighed a great deal, so her movements were restricted, especially in hot weather. With her flamboyant feathered hat, and her hair tied up neatly in a formal bun, this lady is ready for a promenade in the park, taken at a stately and controlled pace with frequent pauses for rest in the shade of the trees.

1920S DOLLS

A 1920s gentleman escorts two flamboyant flappers to an evening dance.

In contrast to the women's style of the period, a man's evening dress of the 1920s was modest and formal with just a few concessions to fashion. The jacket was short cut to the top of well-pressed and creased trousers, accentuating a narrow waistline. A typical pose, often seen in photographs from the time, is of a man with one hand in his trouser pocket and one holding a cigarette, with a reserved—even disdainful—expression on his faces. These young men, with their oiled hair and well-polished shoes, were the perfect foil to their lively flapper partners, who sparkled with laughter and fun.

For women, the 1920s was a period of great freedom, expressed in extrovert fashion and a lively social life. Dorothy Parker, a journalist and witty poet of the period, said: "The playful flapper here we see, the fairest of the fair. She's not what Grandma used to be—you might say 'au contraire'!" Sleek bobbed hair, short-cut skirts, and strings of beads are all hallmarks of the time, for young women fond of an evening's wild dancing and madcap antics. This woman exemplifies flapper style, topped off with a silver lace headdress, a bead-fringed dress, and an ostentatious feather boa.

With a ribbon flower at her shoulder and a low-waisted glittering dress this young woman is ready for an evening out on the town. Dances such as the Charleston were popular, with energetic footwork and a good deal of jumping and hand waving—so flapper dresses were easy to move about in and were low-cut at the neck for flirtatious style. This dress has a metallic thread woven into the fabric, finished with a pretty scalloped edge. Matching jewelry is made from tiny pearlized beads looped into a bracelet and earrings. A strip of colored gauze makes a perfect waistband, set at hip height.

MODERN DOLLS

A family for a modern household wears comfortable and informal clothes.

This man's clothes, typical of the modern era, are designed for casual recreational wear. Comfortable slacks and a loose-fitting sweatshirt allow him to move around, bend, sit, or walk easily—important freedoms of movement that many historical costumes shown in the previous pages would have restricted. Men in contemporary times are far more likely to be involved in domestic family life, so the freedoms to be able to kneel down amid his little daughter's toys, or to join his children in a game of ball in the park, are made possible by his casual and hard-wearing clothes.

In earlier centuries, young girls had little choice about the clothes they wore—much of the decision depended upon the fashion and expectations of the time. Costume tended to reflect a desire for girls to be polite and quiet, and to be seen rather than heard. Little girls in contemporary times are almost spoilt for choice, with special fashions, shoes, and accessories especially designed for them. They are also subject to fewer behavioral restrictions. This little girl has chosen pretty pink tights and a matching dress, with an embroidered motif to reprsent her favorite creature—a beautiful butterfly.

Modern clothes for a regular family are characterized by comfort and an emphasis on the ease of use and movement. The mother in this household has a soft roll-necked sweater machine-knitted from a yarn that has a subtle variegated dye. Modern yarns tend to be made from mixtures of fibers combining qualities of strength and durability. Artificial fibers and dyes are also useful for babies' clothes, for garments that could be washed and washed again, yet still retain their lively coloring. This baby has an all-in-one garment that allows him to learn to crawl and gain early confidence.

SUPPLIERS

Suppliers of craft materials, fabrics, beads, miniature components, dolls, and magazines. Many suppliers can take overseas orders.

UNITED STATES

All About Dolls
72 Lakeside Blvd.
Hopatcong
NJ 07843
USA
Tel: (973) 770 3228
sales@allaboutdolls.com
www.allaboutdolls.com
Thousands of doll-making supplies for porcelain, vinyl, and soft-body dolls.

Dollhouse Miniatures
21027 Crossroads Circle
PO Box 1612
Waukesha
WI 53187-1612
USA
Tel: (800) 446 5489
www.dhminiatures.com

Dolls' House World Magazine
208 Fourth Street SW
Kasson MN 55944
USA
Tel: (507) 634 3143
smalltalk@dollshouseworld.com
www.dollshouseworld.com

The Doll House
6107 N. Scottsdale Road
Scottsdale
AZ 85250
USA
Tel: (480) 948.4630
info@azdollhouse.com
www.azdollhouse.com
Suppliers of dollhouses and accessories.

The Doll Mall
2037 16th Court NE
Issaquah
WA 98029
USA
www.thedollmall.com

The Lawbre Company
888 Tower Road
Mundelein
Illinois 60060
USA
Tel: (800) 253-0491
info@lawbre.com
www.lawbre.com
Suppliers of detailed miniature houses and accessories.

Mott's Miniatures & Doll House Shop
118 East Orangethorpe Avenue
Anaheim
California 92801-1208
USA
Tel: (714) 992-9063
info@mottsminis.com
www.minishop.com

My Doll House
6000 Broadway
Alamo Heights
San Antonio
Texas 78209
USA
Tel: (210) 930-5363
shop@my-dollhouse.com
www.my-dollhouse.com

Nanco Doll Houses
48 East Northfield Avenue
Livingston
NJ 07039
USA
Tel: (973) 992 5858
order@nancodollhouses.com
www.nancodollhouses.com
Building supplies, lighting, and furnishings for dollhouses.

Westcroft Beadworks Inc.
149 Water Street
Norwalk
CT 06854
USA
Tel: (203) 852 9108
mail@beadworks.com
www.beadworks.com
Stores and mail order throughout the USA for beads and jewelry supplies.

UNITED KINGDOM

4D Model Shop
151 City Road
London EC1V 1JH
UK
Tel: (020) 7253 1996
info@modelshop.demon.co.uk
www.modelshop.co.uk
Suppliers of specialist modeling tools and materials, brass fittings, metallic paints, modeling and polymer clay.

Craft Supplies
The Mill
Millers Dale
Buxton
Derbyshire SK17 8SN
UK
Tel: (01298) 871636
sales@craft-supplies.co.uk
www.craft-supplies.co.uk
Shop and mail order for wood, tools, and microtools.

Dainty Supplies Ltd
35 Phoenix Road
Crowther Industrial Estate
(District 3)
Washington NE38 0AD
UK
Tel: (020) 8553 3240
mail@daintysupplies.co.uk
www.daintysupplies.co.uk
Suppliers of pipe cleaners, fur fabric, toy stuffing, felt, ribbons, beads, and sequins.

Dolls' House and Miniature Scene
EMF House
5–7 Elm Park
Ferring
West Sussex BN12 5RN
UK
Tel: (01903) 244900
dolltedemf@aol.com

The Dollshouse Draper
PO Box 128
Lightcliffe
Halifax
West Yorkshire HX3 8RN
UK
Tel: (01422) 201275.
Mail order fabrics, ribbons, lace and trimmings, buttons, beads, eyelets, and buckles

Historical Costume Dolls
35 Lonsdale Way
Oakham
Rutland LE15 6LP
UK
Tel: (01572) 723907
www.costumecavalcade.co.uk
The dolls that appear on pages 136–139 (except for the Shaker doll) were supplied by Historical Costume Dolls.

London Dolls' House Co. Ltd.
29 Covent Garden Market
London WC2E 8RE
UK
Tel: (020) 7240 8681
londondollshouse@amserve.com
www.londondollshouse.co.uk
Suppliers of dollhouse furniture and accessories. Some of their items are featured in this book (details listed on page 144).

Maple Street Museum and Doll's House Shop
Wendy
Royston
Hertfordshire SG8 0AB
UK
Tel: (01223) 207025
info@maplestreet.co.uk
www.maplestreet.co.uk
Suppliers of dollhouse furniture. Some of their furniture is featured on pages 16–19 and pages 80–85.

Paperchase
213 Tottenham Court Road
London W1
UK
Tel: (020) 7467 6200
mailorder@paperchase.co.uk
www.paperchase.co.uk
Suppliers of craft papers, including wood-effect, leather-effect, and brick-effect paper.

Tiranti
27 Warren Street
London W1P 5DG
UK
Tel: (020) 7636 8565
enquiries@tiranti.co.uk
www.tiranti.co.uk
Shop and mail order for specialist tools, knives, art materials, and carving chisels.

AUSTRALIA

The Australian Miniaturist Magazine
PO Box 467
Carlingford
New South Wales 2118
Australia
Tel: (02) 9873 2442

Dollhouse Accessories International
86 Mary Street
Unley, S.A
Australia
Tel: (08) 8271 0311
www.butlerco.com.au/dollhouse

Miniature World Doll House Shop
18 Parkinson Lane
Kardinya
Western Australia 6163
Australia
Tel: (08) 9331 7799
info@MiniatureWorld.com.au
www.miniatureworld.com.au
Suppliers of dollhouses and miniatures.

INDEX

AUTHOR'S ACKNOWLEDGMENTS

Special thanks to Halina Pasierbska and Nick Wise of the Victoria & Albert Museum, to Teresa Thompson of Historical Costume Dolls, to the London Dolls' House Company, to Flick Hart for so kindly acting as Location Manager, and to Joe Short for expert practical assistance with creation of the modern interiors.

CREDITS

Quarto and the author would like to thank and acknowledge the following for supplying pictures reproduced in this book:

The "Tudor banqueting hall" (pages 16–23); "Victorian dining room" (pages 80–87), and "1960s country kitchen" (pages 120–127) are on display at the Maple Street Museum, Wendy, Royston, Hertfordshire SG8 0AB, UK. Tel: 01223 207025; Fax: 01223 207021; Email: info@maplestreet.co.uk; Website: www.maplestreet.co.uk.

The "17th-century lying in room" © Rijksmuseum-Stichting Amsterdam (pages 24–31), is on display at the Rijksmuseum, Stad houderskade 42, 1071 ZD Amsterdam, The Netherlands. Tel: 0031 20 674 7047; Fax: 0031 20 674 7001; Email: info@rijksmuseum.nl; Website: www.rijksmuseum.nl.

The "18th-century merchant's silver room" © Frans Hals Museum, The Netherlands (pages 32–39) is on display at the Frans Hals Museum, Groot Heiligland 62, 2001 DJ Haarlem, The Netherlands. Tel: 0031 23 511 5775; Fax: 0031 23 511 5776; Email: franshalsmuseum@haarlem.nl; Website: www.franshalsmuseum.nl.

The "Chinoiserie sitting room" (pages 48–55) and the "1920s living room" (pages 104–111) both © V&A Picture Library, are on display at the Bethnal Green Museum of Childhood (part of the Victoria & Albert Museum), Cambridge Heath Road, London E2 9PA, UK. Tel: 020 8983 5200; Fax: 020 8983 5225; Email: bgmc@vam.ac.uk; Website: www.vam.ac.uk/vastatic/nmc/.

The "Colonial dining room" (pages 40–47), "American settler's parlor" (pages 72–79), "Old curiosity shop" (pages 64–71), and "Small-town store" (pages 88–95) all reproduced by permission of the American Museum in Britain, Bath ©, are on display at The American Museum in Britain, Claverton Manor, Bath BA2 7BD, UK. Tel: 01225 460503; Fax: 01225 469160; Email: amibbath@aol.com; Website: www.americanmuseum.org.

The "Shaker work room" (pages 58–63) is from a private collection. The miniature Shaker furniture contained in the room was made by John Morgan. Shaker oval boxes (page 61), two-drawer table (pages 57 and 61), peg rail (pages 57 and 59), and hanging shelves (pages 57 and 60) are all available from The Shaker Shop, London, UK. Pictures © Silk Public Relations.

The porcelain replica of a 1950s' Wurlitzer jukebox (pages 112, 113, 118) is from www.americabilia.com.

The "Frank Lloyd Wright sitting room" (pages 96–103), "1950s American diner" (pages 112–119), and "Modern apartment" (pages 128–135) are from the author's own collection.

Apart from the Shaker doll, which is owned by Nick Forder, the dolls on pages 136–139 are all made in 1:12 scale by Teresa Thompson of Historical Costume Dolls, 35 Lonsdale Way, Oakham, Rutland LE15 6LP, UK. Tel: 01572 723907; Website: www.costumecavalcade.co.uk.

Some items of furniture and accessories featured in this book were loaned by the London Dolls' House Company, as follows: Cabinet (pages 24 and 25); "Add to the Look" silverware (page 41); embroidered rug (page 72); sideboard and drop-leaf table (page 73); porcelain and plaster ceiling rose (page 80); dining table (pages 81 and 82); fireplace (page 81); plaster coving (page 84); refrigerator (pages 121 and 123).
For details, contact the London Dolls' House Co. Ltd., 29 Covent Garden Market, London WC2E 8RE, UK. Tel: 020 7240 8681; Fax: 020 7240 2288; Email: londondollshouse@amserve.com; Website: www.londondollshouse.co.uk.

All other photographs and illustrations are the copyright of Quarto. While every effort has been made to credit contributors, we apologize should there have been any omissions or errors.